"This book gives one pause to reflect over what is a serious issue. The concept of an Abundant Quality of Life, as opposed to Abundant 'Stuff,' is something that everyone needs to take heed of. The reminder that The Abundant Life is not free from suffering should make you pause."

Dr. Matthew Crandall,
Dean of Students, Master's International School of Divinity

It was an honor to be asked to copy edit Andre Huynh's book *In Harmony with God*. His understanding and his commitment to God, Jesus, and Christianity come through clearly and will be an inspiration to all who read it.

Herberta Gray,
Copyreader

This book is full of scripture and examples that give us answers to our questions about how to experience the life Jesus promised. It also caused me to evaluate my own commitment. We can live the abundant life Jesus promised!

Diane Hopkins,
Faith Assembly of Lacey, Washington

You have done a wonderful job demonstrating the relevance of the Bible in our life, and I particularly enjoyed the many examples taken both from the Scriptures and from your own experience and observation around you. Your knowledge of the Bible is impressive.

Anne-Cécile,
Indian Christian Fellowship, Puyallup, Washington

in Harmony with God

Andre Huynh

in *Harmony*
with
God

TATE PUBLISHING & *Enterprises*

TATE PUBLISHING
& Enterprises

In Harmony With God
Copyright © 2007 by Andre Huynh. All rights reserved.
This title is also available as a Tate Out Loud audio product.
Visit www.tatepublishing.com for more information.

No part of this publication may be reproduced, stored in a retrieval system or transmitted in any way by any means, electronic, mechanical, photocopy, recording or otherwise without the prior permission of the author except as provided by USA copyright law.

Scripture quotations marked "NKJV" are taken from The New King James Version / Thomas Nelson Publishers, Nashville: Thomas Nelson Publishers. Copyright © 1982. Used by permission. All rights reserved.

Scripture quotations marked "KJV" are taken from the Holy Bible, King James Version, Cambridge, 1769. Used by permission. All rights reserved.

Scripture quotations marked "NIV" are taken from the Holy Bible, New International Version ®, Copyright © 1973, 1978, 1984 by International Bible Society. Used by permission of Zondervan Publishing House. All rights reserved.

The opinions expressed by the author are not necessarily those of Tate Publishing, LLC.

This novel is a work of non-fiction. Several names, descriptions, entities and incidents included in the story are based on the lives of real people.

Book design copyright © 2007 by Tate Publishing, LLC. All rights reserved.
Cover design by Janae J. Glass
Interior design by Chris Webb

Published in the United States of America

ISBN: 1-5988696-1-2
07.01.26

This book is dedicated to:
God the Father, Creator of heaven and the earth;
My Savior, the Lord Jesus Christ;
And the Holy Spirit who enables me to write.

ACKNOWLEDGMENTS

I thank the Lord for my wife for standing by my sides.

I thank the Lord for my children and grandchildren who support me.

I thank the Lord for my brothers and sisters in Christ who pray with me and for me.

I thank the Lord for my teachers and spiritual leaders for their guidance.

TABLE OF CONTENTS

Introduction 15

Chapter I: Blessed Are All Who Fear the Lord 17

Chapter II: God's Presence: The Key to Success 23

Chapter III: God's Will For His People 27

Chapter IV: God's Power in the Universe 41

Chapter V: Where Do We Get Our Power 61

Chapter VI: The Power of the Crowd 71

Chapter VII: Human Weakness 77

Chapter VIII: The Armor of God 83

Chapter IX: Other Powers 89

Chapter X: Men of God 99

Chapter XI: In Christ 139

FOREWORD

Andre Huynh had written "*In Harmony With God*" with one goal in mind and that is to share God's love to others. Andre knows that people who believe and walk faithfully with God can easily attain life's abundance—love, career, relationships, finances. Indeed obeying God's precepts lead to a good and solid future.

As you go through the pages of the book, the verses and scriptures are ones to really pay attention to. Andre took excerpts from both the Old and New Testament, making them alive by examples. In doing so, he awakens sleeping minds and stirs the hearts of both believers and non-believers. The pages put the reader's perspective into motion—that of measuring his own faith. The pages talk of God's essence—omniscient and omnipotent, merciful and kind, forgiving and loving, that He is. As a fellow writer, I find myself learning and relearning about God's commandments. It is a very beautiful walk through for me to read the many inspiring passages on this book. As I read I think of my own walk with God. Am I faithfully following His precepts?

Andre gives the reader a peek of God's ways but most importantly of God's truth and unceasing love. This book is perfect for those who are searching for God and those who want to follow His teachings and be His disciples. I can't help but think of how. Andre has impressively researched the Holy Book and is successful in bringing to our attention God's holiness. Here we regain that special truth of God's unceasing love for us. It is a book good for the soul.

God knew all along where Andre Huynh's talents can be put to use. Andre had used God's gifts successfully. Here he does not need to check our responses or grade our input. He knows exactly that God's words will teach us and bring us the answer to what we need, particularly in searching for that abundant life that He has promised. The story of the master that had given his servants talents is the one that comes to mind at this very moment. Andre is one of those faithful servants. He has used his gifts to teach others.

Andre plans to put the money from the sale of this book to help establish the "Abundant Life Ministry" in Vietnam and also to support local Vietnamese churches.

"In Harmony with God" speaks of God's truth. The pages are littered with scriptures and verses to address and explain God's truth. As a writer, I find myself, measuring my own awareness of God's blessings.

On a personal note: Thank you, Andre, for such an inspiring book! Allow me to share some lines from the poem I wrote since it reminds me of you and your ways. (*Excerpts from "I Will Always Be That"*).

"I will do things my Lord, the way You want me to
I will talk and walk righteously, as I represent You
I will use my gifts, my Lord, the ones You want me to share
I am Your servant, Lord, now and forever!"

Virginia Deferia
"My Hands In His"
Gleams of Hope

INTRODUCTION

Last year I studied Contemporary Theology, and I found Success Theology interesting. Of course, all of the Lord Jesus' teachings are great, and need to be remembered and put into practice. He stated, *"The thief comes only to steal and kill and destroy; I have come that they may have life, and have it to the full"* (John 12:12). That is one of the favorite scriptures of the Success advocates. It is also one of my favorite scriptures because I want that kind of life. I myself love and enjoy an abundant life that He intends for me.

Then it dawned on me that I should study how to be victorious as a Christian. I began to write down what I have learned in order to share with those who are asking the Lord why their lives are so miserable. I wish that the Lord would reveal to me everything I need to know to be victorious so I may share with you His secret. Unfortunately, I'm not a spiritual giant. I have dug into His spiritual mine, and have found some helpful principles we can apply in our lives, so that we will be happier and less miserable. Another purpose for this book is to raise funds for *Abundant Life Ministry*. The money that comes from the sale of the book will be used to support Vietnamese Local Churches in Vietnam. I've seen many Christians and Ministers struggling with finances. When their basic needs are not met, they can't dedicate their lives to God's service. I do not consider myself as a gifted author, but a servant. I'd use the tenth of a talent that the Lord has given me to make a tiny difference to my brothers and sisters in Vietnam.

Many years ago I watched a video that teaches us about how to make a difference in the life of others. A man walks along a beach, picking up starfish and throwing them back to the sea. A person passing by asks him, "What are you doing?" "I'm trying to save the lives of these small animals," the man replies, "because they will dry out and die when the sun comes up." The man walking by says, "There are many of them, how can you save them all?" The man picks another starfish, throws it back into the water, and says, "At least I can make a difference for this guy." I cannot make a difference to all Vietnamese, but the Lord's will for my wife and me is to use what He gives to us to assist some whom we meet on our path.

1

Blessed are all who fear the Lord

The Lord God spoke to Moses, *"Now if you obey me fully and keep my covenant, then out of all nations you will be my treasured possession. Although the whole earth is mine, you will be for me a kingdom of priests and a holy nation. These are the words you are to speak to the Israelites"* (Exodus 19:5–6). The Scripture tells us how the covenant was made. In the above covenant, Sovereign God declares what He will do for Israel upon the condition that the Israelites accept His will. God makes very clear that His people will receive His blessings when they fully obey all His commands, and be cursed, if they don't. He commands them not to bow down to idols and worship them. He will punish the children for the sin of the fathers to the third and fourth generation. But, He will show love to a thousand generations of those who love Him and keep His commandments (Deuteronomy 20:6).

Psalm 128 expresses the same truth for today as in Biblical times, and the truth is that all who fear the Lord, and who walk in

His ways will be blessed and prosper. On the contrary, the wicked, or those who do not fear the Lord will only exist.

That truth is like a thread going through the Old Testament.

Moses was called to deliver God's people from slavery in Egypt. At first, he was hesitant due to the lack of confidence. But, after the Lord had promised that He would be with Moses, the man of God followed all of the Lord's instructions. The Lord performed mighty deeds through Moses. However, in the first month, when the Israelites arrived in the desert of Zin, there was no water. The community protested against Moses and Aaron. The Lord showed up and instructed Moses to speak to a rock so that it would pour out its water. But, instead of speaking to that rock, Moses struck the rock twice with his staff. Thus, Moses made one mistake, and was not allowed to enter the Promised Land, *"But the LORD said to Moses and Aaron, 'Because you did not trust in me enough to honor me as holy in the sight of the Israelites, you will not bring this community into the land I give them'"* (Numbers 20:12).

After Moses had passed away, the Lord appointed Joshua, his assistant, to lead the Israelites. He would cross the Jordan River, and possess the Land that the Lord had promised to Abraham approximately five hundred years before. God reminded Joshua of the Mosaic Covenant, *"Be careful to obey all the law my servant Moses gave you; do not turn from it to the right or to the left, that you may be successful wherever you go"* (Joshua 1:7).

If Moses was a great political leader, Joshua was a great military leader. The Bible tells us of his exploits, *"So Joshua took the entire land, just as the LORD had directed Moses, and he gave it as an inheritance to Israel according to their tribal divisions. Then the land had rest from war"* (Joshua 11:23). The Israelites under Joshua's leadership defeated thirty-one kings in all.

Their enemies were defeated when they were in tune with

God. He was the One who drew out the plan of the attack of Jericho. Even though the Israelites did not fully understand how that plan would work, but they followed His plan, and saw the walls of Jericho tumble down.

Before Jericho fell, God's people were told:

> "*The city and all that is in it are to be devoted to the LORD… But keep away from the devoted things, so that you will not bring about your own destruction by taking any of them. Otherwise you will make the camp of Israel liable to destruction and bring trouble on it. All the silver and gold and the articles of bronze and iron are sacred to the LORD and must go into his treasury*"
> (Joshua 6:17—19).

But the Israelite acted unfaithfully in regard to devoted things. Achan, son of Carmi of the tribe of Judah took some of them. "*So the LORD's anger burned against Israel*" (Joshua 7:1). That was because they did not obey the Lord their God. Right then, God's people should have made peace with the Lord. Unfortunately they moved on, and tried to attack the next city, Ai.

Thirty-six men died because Achan "*has violated the covenant of the LORD and has done a disgraceful thing in Israel*" (Joshua 7:15—NIV)!

Only after the sinner and his family had been punished the Israelites captured Ai and set it on fire.

The above narrative was an illustration of the harmony with God.

When the Israelites did not have kings, and lead by the Judges, the people turned from their true King and Lord. The Book of Judges described the history of Israel as repeated cycles: apostasy, slavery, repentance, and deliverance.

In a Vietnamese Weekly Newspaper, Vietbao USA, issue #491, there was an article concerning the Chinese population. A quarter of a century ago, the Chinese government adopted a "One Child per Family" policy which resulted in a decrease in its population, particularly the number of born females. Currently, in 2005, the President of the Communist Party blames the government for the decrease in the Chinese population. Also the number of females has been decreasing drastically, due to the Chinese culture that prefers boys to girls. The government's policy and the culture have contributed to the abortion of the female fetus. The President called for a meeting of three hundred demographers. They suggested that he had better stop enforcing "One Child per Family" policy.

Many years ago, in China, the sparrow population increased considerably. The government encouraged the farmers to kill all the sparrows. Years later, there were not enough birds to control the mass of insects that destroyed the crops.

In the United States last year, a cougar attacked and killed a cyclist on a trail, down in California. That accident would not have happened if animal lovers had not over-protected the deer population in that area. The deer that roamed around that trail attracted the cougar, which in turn attacked people instead of deer.

The above information indicates that the Lord created all living creatures, and He equipped them with a balancing system.

If there were a better birth control management, education, and policy, China could control the population growth rate effectively. Before the government stepped in and tried to control the population growth, the people of China had more females than males. Now, after twenty-five year of birth control, China does not have enough females.

In the U.S.A. two hot issues are dividing the U.S. Congress

and the State Legislatures: abortion and same sex-marriage. When God says something immoral, then it is immoral. There is no need to argue. In many countries Legislatures are silent about those issues. That is understandable since they do not recognize the Bible as their moral value or legal standard. In those countries people are free to kill babies or to practice homosexuality. Also in those countries the government does not pay for abortion, nor issue permits for gay-marriage. The government may not put in jail the women who aborts or two men or two women living together as husband and wife. But tax money should not be used for abortion, and marriage licenses should not be issued to same sex couples.

Recently the physicians in the State of New York discovered in the blood of a man a variant HIV virus that no one has seen before. There is no cure for this new kind of virus. Thomas Frieden, an official of the New York Department of Health stated, "We have never seen such a case. It is a serious threat to the public health." The virus was found in a man who admitted he was homosexual. That is understandable, since it is written, "*God cannot be mocked. A man reaps what he sows.*" That man chose a lifestyle that was not in tune with God; so he suffered its consequence. I would like to add that not all who are HIV positive are homosexual. But, a homosexual more likely contracts Aids.

God not only creates the universe, He also sustains it, and keeps it in check. When man tries to go against God's system, chaos will follow. A Vietnamese proverb teaches, "If we go along with God's will, we will survive; if we go against God's will, we surely die." That was what the Lord warned Adam and Eve of, "*You are free to eat from any tree in the garden, but you must not eat from the tree of the knowledge of good and evil, for when you eat of it you will surely die*" (Genesis 2:16–17).

Hezekiah was one of the good kings of Judah. The Bible tells us, *"Hezekiah trusted in the LORD, the God of Israel. There was no one like him among all the kings of Judah, either before him or after him. He held fast to the LORD and did not cease to follow him; he kept the commands the LORD had given Moses. And the LORD was with him; he was successful in whatever he undertook. He rebelled against the king of Assyria and did not serve him"* (2 Kings 18:5–8).

The key phrase is, "the Lord was with him." If the Lord was with Hezekiah, no one can be against him. In a matter of fact, even Sennacherib, the mighty king of Assyria could not touch Hezekiah (2 Kings 18 & 19).

Second Kings 18 also informs us that in King Hezekiah's fourth year, Shalmaneser king of Assyria marched against Samaria and laid siege to it, and at the end of three years the Assyrians took it. So Samaria was captured in Hezekiah's sixth year, and the king of Assyria deported Israel to Assyria. The Scripture says, *"This happened because they had not obeyed the LORD their God, but had violated his covenant-all that Moses the servant of the LORD commanded. They neither listened to the commands nor carried them out"* (2 Kings 18:12).

The Lord handed the king and the people of Israel over to the Assyrians because they were not in harmony with the Holy One of Israel. But Hezekiah was saved because he trusted in the Lord, and held fast to God.

"Draw near to God and He draws near to you."

2

God's Presence: The Key to Success

Abraham is known as a great man of faith. He was credited as righteous just because of his faith, and with his faith he became the ancestor of all Christians. Even though he did not prove himself as perfect, no one would say, "Abraham was not a great man." His greatness did not come from himself. We may say that the presence of the Lord makes his name great.

Abraham built an altar to the Lord because he was aware of the presence of God.

Today, we Christians still need to set apart a place to meet with God. Many Christian Churches do not have an altar for the Lord, but believers still need a building for corporate worship. The Lord Jesus promises to His followers, *"For where two or three come together in my name, there am I with them"* (Matthew 18:20).

Through the Lord Jesus Christ all believers may have access to the throne of God anytime and anywhere, *"Let us then approach the throne of grace with confidence, so that we may receive mercy and find grace to help us in our time of need* (Hebrews 4:16). Then can we be sure that "When we are in God's presence, His grace can help us in our time of need." We can be rest assured on that promise, because we know that He is faithful to fulfill His promise, and because He loves us so much. If one may take hold of God's grace, or of His power, then how much grace and power can an assembly receive?

The Book of Chronicles is filled with interesting stories, and that of king Asa deserves our attention. There were not many godly kings in Judah, but Asa was a good king. He did not worship idols, he instead commanded his people to seek the Lord their God, and to obey Him. He also removed the high places and incense altars in every town in Judah, and therefore, the kingdom was at peace under him (II Chronicles 14:5).

When Zerah the Cushite, with his vast army attacked Judah, king Asa knew his weakness, and called the Lord for help. The king admitted that Zerah was mightier than he, so he prayed, "*Help us, O LORD our God, for we rely on you, and in your name we have come against this vast army. O LORD, you are our God; do not let man prevail against you*" (2 Chronicles 14:11). The rest of chapter 14 tells us that the Lord struck down the Cushites before Asa and Judah, and the men of Judah carried home a large amount of plunder.

Chapter 15 teaches us a great lesson. The first part of the chapter tells us Azariah son of Oded went out to meet Asa and said to him, "*Listen to me, Asa and all Judah and Benjamin. The LORD is with you when you are with him. If you seek him, he will be found by you, but if you forsake him, he will forsake you*" (2 Chronicles 15:1–3).

Those verses were written approximately 2900 years ago, but they are still true today. The Lord Jesus teaches that not everyone who calls Him 'Lord' will enter the kingdom of heaven because

He did not know that person. He never sought or never was with Jesus. According to the word of Azariah son of Oded, the Lord is with anyone who is with Him. Anyone who seeks the Lord with all his heart will find Him, "*You will seek me and find me when you seek me with all your heart*" (Jeremiah 29:13–14).

At the end of chapter 22 of the Book of Chronicles, we learn that after the death of king Ahaziah, Athaliah, the king's mother proceeded to destroy the whole royal family of the house of Judah. But Jehosheba, the king's sister managed to take away Joash, the king's son, and put him and his nurse in a bedroom. Because Jehosheba was the wife of the priest Jehoiada, Joash remained hidden in the temple of God for six years while Athaliah ruled the land. Those years were the only period of time that the throne of David fell into the hands of a stranger since the death of Solomon.

II Chronicles 23 narrated the coup of the priest Jehoiada to dethrone Athaliah, and to crown Joash king of Judah. Chapter 24 described how the king ordered his people to bring their contributions to rebuild the temple of God according to its original design.

However, after the death of Jehoiada, king Joash lost spiritual guidance, and listened to the officials of Judah who were not godly.

> "*They abandoned the temple of the LORD, the God of their fathers, and worshiped Asherah poles and idols. Because of their guilt, God's anger came upon Judah and Jerusalem. Although the LORD sent prophets to the people to bring them back to him, and though they testified against them, they would not listen*"
> (2 Chronicles 24:18–19).

The Spirit of God spoke through Zachariah son of Jehoiada the priest, *"You will not prosper. Because you have forsaken the LORD, he has forsaken you"* (2 Chronicles 24:20). But king Joash did not heed the warning of the Lord; he killed the man of God instead. Therefore God led the king and the leaders of people into the hand of the army of Aram although the Aramean army had come with only a few men.

From the history of Judah recorded in the book of Second Chronicles we have learned that "If we go along with God's will, we will survive, if we go against God's will, we shall surely die."

In the last couple of weeks in June 2005 an assistant Chief of Staff of the President of the United States has been under fire because he could not be silent on something. He should not have disclosed to the media the name of the secret agent. If I did what he did I would be in jail. However, he is an asset to the current Administration, so he was not fired. The TV reporters label him as "untouchable."

Spiritually speaking no one is untouchable, since we are all sinners, and come short of the glory of God. And as such we could not escape the death penalty. However, if we are in Christ, He already paid for our sins, we are not cast out of God's presence, we are untouchable, as God's word has promised, *"Therefore, there is now no condemnation for those who are in Christ Jesus, because through Christ Jesus the law of the Spirit of life set me free from the law of sin and death"* (Romans 8:1).

3

God's Will for His People

        an we know God's will? I have heard some Christians say "Yes," while many may answer "No," or "I am not sure." I, myself, do not easily believe a person when he [1] states that he heard from God. Only the Lord and that person know.

    According to the Bible God created Adam and Eve. The Lord himself visited the couple, maybe every day, as recorded in the book of Genesis, *"Then the man and his wife heard the sound of the LORD God as he was walking in the garden in the cool of the day, and they hid from the LORD God among the trees of the garden"* (Genesis 3:8).

    Therefore the Lord must have communicated with them everyday. What did they talk about? The Bible does not tell us, but the following verses reveal His will for mankind:

    To take care of his creation, to *"rule over the fish of the sea and the birds of the air, over the livestock, over all the earth, and over all the creatures that move along the ground"* (Genesis 1:26).[2]

    To multiply and fill the earth (1:28).[3]

    The above information gives us an idea of what the Lord discussed daily with the first couple. He may have taught Adam how to take good care of his entire creation, because "he saw that it was good." He may have taught the couple how to build a strong family if they would let him be their marriage Counselor.

He also told them that they were free to eat from any tree in the garden, but they must not eat from the tree of the knowledge of good and evil, for when they eat of it they will surely die (Genesis 2:16–17).

The above information tells us that Adam and Eve were very close to their Creator, and they knew exactly what He expected from them. It is very critical that we listen to Him and do exactly what He commands.

Something else we have learned from the above narrative is a person can know God's will as long as he keeps a close personal relationship with Him.

Before Adam and Eve disobeyed God—we call it the Fall of man—they had enjoyed an abundant life, a quality life as the Lord had intended for them.

After the Fall, they lost all their privileges, and through them sin entered the world. When communication is cut off, people can hardly hear from God. The story of the *"Prodigal son"* recorded in the Book of Luke is a good illustration of the loss of privileges and quality life due to the separation from the Heavenly Father.

In that account, the younger son, when he was still at home, did not realize that he could access to his father's riches, he did not realize that his father's assets were available to him. The fact that his father gave him his inheritance in a lump sum implied that his father would provide all his needs. His father would provide him more than what he asked for. The son would have been better off to ask for a little bit at a time as long as his father was still alive. However, as soon as he took his share in a lump sum, what he had did not last for a long time, and he became empty-handed.

Through that parable the Lord Jesus wanted us to know that as long as we remain in Him, we may draw upon His abundant resource. He has promised to us, *"You may ask me for anything in my name, and I will do it"* (John 14:14). When the Son of God promises something, we can rest assured that He will do it, because He is faithful, like God the Father.

Sin cuts off communication between God and man. Man does not know his Creator, and His will. Fortunately, God provided man with His word, so that, at least, we may know His will in general. That will is stated by the Lord Jesus, *"I have come that they may have life, and have it to the full"* (John 10:10).

For God so loves those He created, He came into the world of sinners and lived as a human being so that we *"may have life, and have it in full,"* meaning we can live successfully.

Do you know how many Christians have enjoyed that kind of life, or were just barely hanging in there? I don't know. However, we can agree that there are a lot of Christians who know that they are saved "by faith, through grace," and we also know that many of our brothers and sisters are saved, *"But only as one escaping through the flames"* (1 Corinthians 3:15).

My sister was converted to Christianity by marriage. She took on her husband's religion. She attends Church services regularly, says prayers in Church services. But, I've never heard her sharing what the Lord had done for her; she never witnessed to me, and asked if I wish to have Christ as Lord and Savior. That tells me that she is never excited about God. The Lord blessed her financially with her deceased husband's pension, but I don't think her life is fulfilling. Because she believes in the Lord Jesus Christ, she will be with Him in heaven, but *"as one escaping through the flames."* Yet, I love her because the Lord Jesus loves her.

I am one of the many who believes in eternal security, or that, once we are saved, we will not lose our salvation, as our Lord Jesus promises, *"I give them eternal life, and they shall never perish; no one can snatch them out of my hand. My Father, who has given them to me, is greater than all; no one can snatch them out of my Father's hand"* (John 10:27–29). I know that Christians would not lose their salvation, even though sometime they wandered away from the Lord.

I have been obsessed by the issue of how to live a victorious life, as the Lord Jesus declared in John 10:10. Recently, I received a piece of revelation that helped me to understand the key to an abundant life. By that, I do not mean that I have it yet, but, borrowing the word of the apostle Paul, *"Not that I have already obtained all this, or have already been made perfect"* (Philippians 3:12).

What I am attempting to do is to share the information I received, so that we can enjoy an abundant life on the earth. The ultimate goal of a Christian is to seek first the kingdom of God and His righteousness, but, not to live a miserable life on the earth, *"I have come that they may have life, and have it to the full (John 10:10).*

The same promise was also found in the Old Testament, *"For I know the plans I have for you," declares the LORD, "plans to prosper you and not to harm you, plans to give you hope and a future. Then you will call upon me and come and pray to me, and I will listen to you* (Jeremiah 29:11–12).

What we don't understand is why some Christians fail to enjoy that kind of life. Is God not faithful? No, because the Bible affirms that He is. If so, it is our fault, and how do we receive that abundant life? It seems to me that we need some kind of power.

The Bible teaches, *"For since the creation of the world God's invisible qualities-his eternal power and divine nature-have been clearly seen, being understood from what has been made, so that men are without excuse"* (Romans 1:20).

That's right, *"his eternal power and divine nature have been seen"* in the universe, and it is available to us. I believe that, if we can access to His divine power, we will have a victorious life, both in the physical realm and in the spiritual realm.

Abundant Life

Since the first married couple on the earth looked at the fruit that was pleasant to the eye, and good to eat, man has been so caught up with the "the cravings of sinful man, the lust of his eyes." The majority of human beings try to attain an abundant life in terms of money and material goods. But what does the Lord try to say?

The Lord Jesus asks His disciple, *"For what profit is it to a man if he gains the whole world, and loses his own soul? Or what will a man give in exchange for his soul?"* (Matthew 16:26–27—NKJV). To Him, the soul of a person is more important than what he owns.

On another occasion, someone in the crowd asks the Lord Jesus to be an arbiter between him and his brother who did not divide the inheritance with him. After rebuking that man, *"Then he said to them, "Watch out! Be on your guard against all kinds of greed; a man's life does not consist in the abundance of his possessions"* (Luke 12:15).

The Lord took that occasion to tell the crowd a parable. There was a rich man who was blessed with abundant crop. He planned to tear down his barns, and build bigger barns. *"But God said to him, 'You fool! This very night your life will be demanded from you. Then who will get what you have prepared for yourself?'"* (Luke 12:20).

According to the Lord Jesus' teaching "life in abundance" does not mean material prosperity, but quality life. I am not against prosperity. On the contrary I love to be rich. Paul urges the thief not to steal, but to work hard to have more than enough, so that he can share with the needy.

In the Old Testament we see people whom the Lord God

blessed with great riches like Job, Abraham, Lot, Isaac, and Jacob. Even though Jacob was the son of a rich man, he was penniless when he fled to Mesopotamia. Twenty years later he returned home with "cattle and donkeys, sheep and goats, menservants and maidservants."

One of God's Names is Jehovah Jireh, the Lord provides. We don't know why one has more than the other, but as one psalmist testifies, *"I was young and now I am old, yet I have never seen the righteous forsaken or their children begging bread"* (Psalm 37:25).

The apostle Paul was one of the great men in Christ. Who would say he did not have a good life? Yet, we know through his epistle to the Philippians that sometimes he experienced poverty, *"I know what it is to be in need, and I know what it is to have plenty. I have learned the secret of being content in any and every situation, whether well fed or hungry, whether living in plenty or in want"* (Philippians 4:12).

"Being content," that's the key of an abundant life. The righteous people are not forsaken, and their children do not need to beg for bread. They may not have plenty of bread, but they can be, like Paul, content. It is a life full of "love, joy, peace, patience, kindness, goodness, faithfulness, gentleness and self-control" (Galatians 5:22). It's a life abiding in Christ, and filled with the Holy Spirit.

Just like Jeremiah the prophet, Samson was set apart even before he was born to deliver Israel from the hands of the Philistines. Unfortunately, Samson did not, like Paul, do one thing, that was to press on toward the goal to win the prize for which God had called him. Instead, Samson had his mind set on what his flesh desired. Consequently, he did not live an abundant life as Deborah or Gideon. Physically speaking, Samson might have had great times with his girlfriends, but in the spiritual his life was not really as successful as the Lord wanted it to be.

Last year a lady who has claimed to be prophetess got married. She spent approximately one million dollars for her wedding. I do not say that was wrong or right because the word of God does not tell me. What I know is many Old Testament prophets were not rich, and they did not beg for bread. 2 Kings 5 records the story of Naaman, commander of the army of the king of Aram. Naaman was healed from leprosy with the help of Elishah. To show his appreciation Naaman wished to compensate Elishah with gold, silver and clothes. The prophet told the Commander, "*As surely as the LORD lives, whom I serve, I will not accept a thing.*" And even though Naaman urged him, he refused (2 Kings 5:16). Perhaps Elishah did not accept the gift because he did not heal the man, and also, because the Lord was his shepherd, and he was not in need.

Let's now move to our time, March of 2005. This morning most, if not all, TV and radio stations announced the prison release of Martha Stewart. Martha, who made millions selling housekeeping advice and accessories, was convicted of lying about investments and of doing something else I did not know. As all know-maybe not fifty years from now-Martha herself is a success story.

Only the Lord God knows whether Martha was sentenced justly or unjustly. According to Krysten Crawford: "Stewart, 63, could have stayed out of prison, possibly for good, if she had waited until a court ruled on her still-pending appeal. But she said last fall that she wanted to put the nearly three-year-old ordeal behind her, both for her sake and for that of her company, which has been bleeding money because of her." [4]

However, in that entire unfortunate situation Martha kept a good attitude. Crawford reported, "In her statement early Friday, Stewart said she will 'never forget' the women she met in prison—

all that they have done to help me over these five months, their children, and the stories they have told me."

She is also blessed, continued Crawford, "Unlike most people just out of prison, Stewart won't have to pound the pavement looking for a job. Even before her release, NBC announced it would air a daily Martha show, plus appearances twice a month on the 'Today show.' At the same time, she will be filming a new version of 'The Apprentice,' where she will give people the ax in her own inimitable style."

I think Martha must have put her trust in some Supernatural Being to keep her high in the spirit. As for me I need His strength as the psalmist says, *"I love you, O LORD, my strength. The LORD is my rock, my fortress and my deliverer; my God is my rock, in which I take refuge. He is my shield and the horn of my salvation, my stronghold"* (Ps 18:1–2).

In an issue of the VietBao Daily News, March 4, 2005, there is an article entitled "Two-Way Measurement." It says, "On the graph representing American assets from WWII, the line is going up sharply. The annual income per capita has tripled. Houses are larger every day. On the other hand, on the graph representing happiness of Americans, the line has been on the same level for the last sixty years. In 1950, a survey conducted by the National Research Center indicated that one third of Americans are happy. That number has not changed.

"When we look at the graph showing the people who suffer depression we will see that there are from three to ten times more people depressed than before." We may ask "People today have more money in their pockets, why are they are less happy?"

The article explains, "We spend a lot of time and energy seeking the things money can buy such as houses and cars, and do not get involved in contributing to the well-being of others such as helping the needy, developing friendships, and nurturing spiritual life. Many people think that shopping for expensive items is the shortcut to happiness, a psychologist from the University of Pennsylvania says."

The article goes on to say, "In a recent survey conducted by Time Magazine, the degree of happiness rises with the annual income level up to fifty thousand dollars. Thereafter, income no longer has any influence. Diener, a sociologist from the University of Illinois, interviewed four hundred rich people listed on Forbes 400, and concluded that they are happier than an average person, but not that much. The reason is that rich people are still envious of prosperity and of popularity." [5]

Religious men or women can practice happiness regardless of their social status or financial security. The average person requires extra grace from the Mighty King Jesus. The word of God cites thousands of ways of being happy, but it does not guarantee happiness to rich men. Happiness is promised to:

"The man who does not walk in the counsel of the wicked, or stand in the way of sinners, or sit in the seat of mockers" (Psalm 1:1).

"The man whose sin the LORD does not count against him and in whose spirit is no deceit" (Psalm 32:2).

Christian is a pilgrim, he is on a journey, and God's purpose is for us to enjoy our trip. Spiritual growth will help us to receive His entire blessing.

Paul gives the Christians in Colossae the key to a good spiritual journey,

- *Set your minds on things above, not on earthly things* (Colossians 3:2).
- *Put to death, therefore, whatever belongs to your earthly nature: sexual immorality, impurity, lust, evil desires and greed, which is idolatry* (3:5).
- *But now you must rid yourselves of all such things as these: anger, rage, malice, slander, and filthy language from your lips* (3:8).

The soul is deep, it is below the level of a conscious awareness, and it is the foundation of who I am. If I neglect my soul, various aspects of my life will be affected, and I can't enjoy life. In order to have a healthy soul, I must:

1) Be strongly connected with God, the source of strength, *"He gives strength to the weary and increases the power of the weak"* (Isaiah 40:29).

2) Be receptive to God, *"I am the vine; you are the branches. If a man remains in me and I in him, he will bear much fruit; apart from me you can do nothing"* (John 15:5).

Abundant Life Is Not Free From Suffering

Satan, since the fall of man, is always hostile to the seed of the woman who is the Lord Jesus. And because he hates Jesus, he also hates His children, or Christians. He always goes after the followers of Christ.

The battle is real. Christians are believers of Christ, and also soldiers of Christ. In politics, one may be neither rightist nor leftist. But in the spiritual realm, one must take a side, either for Christ or against Him. When we are for Christ we expect to be persecuted because of him. The Lord Jesus has warned us, *"If the world hates you, keep in mind that it hated me first"* (John 15:18).

Today, two thousand years after Jesus was crucified, every hour seventeen Christians lay down their lives for the sake of Jesus Christ. A fulfilled life may be filled with trials and tribulations, but it is a blessed life according to the Lord's word, *"Blessed are you when people insult you, persecute you and falsely say all kinds of evil against you because of me"* (Matthew 5:11).

We learn from the book of Acts the story of Paul and Silas. They were falsely accused of throwing the city of Philippi into an uproar. The magistrates ordered them to be stripped, flogged, and thrown into prison. They were put in the inner cell and their feet fastened in the stocks. But, instead of having a pity party, they celebrated the Lord. They were praying and singing hymns to God. Their prayers and praises touched the heart of God. Suddenly a violent earthquake shook the prison, and the prison doors flew open. Paul and Silas didn't escape as criminals; they stayed calm instead. Paul's faith and Silas' faith not only delivered them, but also saved the jailer and his family. The blessed life of Christians does affect the life of others.

I had time to watch Michael Jackson's verdict, and the verdict was "not guilty." TV reporters said there would be a celebration at Mr. Jackson's ranch that night. In a matter of fact, the Bible says, *"Blessed is the man whose sin the LORD does not count against him and in whose spirit is no deceit"* (Psalm 32:2).

A man who is in Christ Jesus, or who is united with Him, is a blessed man for he is no longer condemned, and God is with him. If we learn His truth, and obey His teaching, we live the abundant life He intends for us. But the life on this earth is temporal. The ultimate life is the one we will spend with Him for eternity.

Abundant Life People

In different countries, at different times, there has been a "model person," an exemplary person whom people admire, and want to be like.

The 19th century "gentleman" knew how to act properly in public, how to deal with others, how to comport himself as a gentleman. The following insert gives us a picture of a gentleman:

> "Colonel Grangerford was a gentleman you see. He was a gentleman all over...His hands was long and

thin, and every day of his life he put on a clean shirt and a full suit from head to foot made out of linen so white it hurt your eyes to look at it; and on Sunday he wore a blue tail-coat and brass buttons on it...There weren't no frivolishness about him, not a bit, and he weren't never loud"
 —Adventures of Huckleberry Finn, Mark Twain

In the 17th century the model man in France was called a "honnête homme." He was similar to an English gentleman, and could discuss different subjects. He was a nice person to talk to.

In 5 b.c. Confucius wrote and taught his philosophy that today we call Confucianism. Confucius' model man was called a "chun tzu," literally meaning "son of the king." He knew how to keep his three relationships in check: with the king, with his wife and with his son. Besides, he needed to practice the five fundamental moral values: "Ren" or kindness; "Ye" or righteousness; "Li" or profit, gain, advantage: NOT a proper motive for action affecting others; "Li" or good manner, worship; "Yi" or conscientiousness and loyalty.

Above are some "model men." They are good men, maybe happy men, but their lives may not be abundant.

In the U.S, Television reporters have called popular singers "American idols." Truly, young Americans are very fond of their idols to the point they worship them. At concerts the music fans yell their heads off, raised theirs hands, and they are almost ready to die for their idols. I was the same. As a teen, even though I did not live in the U.S., I loved Elvis Presley, Paul Anka, Pat Boone.

Now, I admire the men of God. They are not my idols, but the ones I look up to as spiritual models. After the Lord Jesus, and the apostles, I want to be like them.

One of them is the late Pastor G. Vernon McGee. His last

church was in Pasadena, California, USA. He was called to teach the Bible through the radio. He was faithful to his calling. He passed away many years ago, but people can still learn from him. His teaching is still on the air. That is truly abundant life in Christ Jesus. Pastor McGee is no more, but his teaching still lives on. He went through the Bible in five years and explained God's word.

My other model is the greatest evangelist of all time, Dr. Billy Graham. At the age of 86—in 2005—Reverend Graham, even he is not physically well, he finished his last crusade in the great City of New York with a crowd of eighty thousand people. He started his first crusade in 1947. For fifty-eight long years Dr. Graham has faithfully preached the gospel with one message: "Jesus saves." Maybe a million people all over the world responded to his call, and received Christ as their Lord and Savior. Their lives have changed for good. He was honored many times, but was not rich like many other preachers.

The key to Dr. Graham's success is his faithfulness to the call, his passion for God's business, his focus on one thing, and his ability to do all things through Christ who strengthens him. I know that you know many other "model men or women," but those two men impress me the most.

4

God's Power in the Universe

That's right, the Lord God is omniscient, but He does not recognize us if we do not acknowledge Him as Lord.

The Lord Jesus teaches, "Not everyone who says to me, 'Lord, Lord,' will enter the kingdom of heaven, but only he who does the will of my Father who is in heaven" (Matthew 7:21). Is it sad? Doing the will of the Father matters much to Him. As a matter of fact, whoever is doing God's will is His mother and His brothers.

When we see Him face to face, we would like to hear Him say, "Ye good and faithful servant." That is really meaningful. The Bible mentions different crowns as the rewards for God's servants: the crown of life, the crown of joy, and the crown of glory. But the ultimate crown is his commendation, "Ye good and faithful servant."

Draw near to God in order to know His will, and to do His will, and to hear Him say, "I know you." That will be the best reward for any followers of Jesus Christ. His presence is sufficient, just as His grace is sufficient in our discomfort. It is very beneficial to Christians to draw near to the Heavenly Father because He owns all the power we need.

Through one psalmist the Lord declares, "For I am the LORD your God, who churns up the sea so that its waves roar—the LORD Almighty is his name . . . I who set the heavens in place, who laid the foundations of the earth, and who say to Zion, 'You are my people.'" (Isaiah 51:15–16). When one is born, that knowledge is loaded in his heart. Someone becomes an atheist because he chooses to do so, or he listens to a lie.

In 2004 the State of Florida was hit three times by hurricanes that destroyed thousand of homes. In the same year tsunamis killed approximately three hundred thousand people in Asia. That did not include many thousand others who died from diseases related to the disaster.

Those facts are a few of the demonstrations of the power on the earth. When we move out of our planet, we cannot imagine the greatness of that power.

In "The Collapse of Evolution," Scott M. Huse wrote, "The energy given off by our sun has been computed to equal that of a billion hydrogen bombs being detonated every second. Some stars are so large and bright that they radiate energy anywhere from 100,000 to 1 million times as fast as our own sun!"[6] That is power. And where did that tremendous power come from? We may not agree on whether or not God misuses His power to generate hurricanes, tsunamis and other disasters. But we can agree that He is the owner of all the resources to create and to run the universe, and He does that well.

Let's think of the sun, "*It never hurries, never gets excited, it just works slowly and makes no noise—doesn't push any buzzers, doesn't answer any telephones, just goes on shining, and the sun does more work in a fraction of an instant than you and I could ever do in a lifetime. Think of what it does. It causes the flowers to bloom, keeps the trees growing, warms the earth, causes the fruit and vegetables to grow and the crops to ripen, lifts water to send back to the earth, and it makes you feel* 'peaceful like'"[7] If scientists knew how to tap on the immeasurable energy of the sun, people would greatly benefit from that huge resource. The best deal is that the energy of the sun is free.

The Bible tells us that, even though God is invisible, He has prepared everything for human beings to enjoy a good life on the earth. However:

> *"For although they knew God, they neither glorified him as God nor gave thanks to him, but their thinking became futile and their foolish hearts were darkened. Although they claimed to be wise, they became fools and exchanged the glory of the immortal God for images made to look like mortal man and birds and animals and reptiles."*
> (Romans 1:21–23)

So men are without excuses.

In the morning, if I want breakfast, I have to crack the egg, fry it, and toast the bread. The cooking, however simple it is, takes time and energy. I cannot just command the egg to be fried, the bread to be toasted, so that my breakfast is ready in a split-second.

The sun does what is assigned to it. It does it easily, and effectively.

My weakness is that I like to finish a task as quickly as I can. When I eat, it does not take me long to finish my meal. Thank God, I do not have problem with my stomach. But, I always remind myself to slow down, to take time to chew, to make sure that my stomach will not spend more energy to digest the foods.

This morning I had a few minutes to watch a match of pool. The woman playing really took time to play. She observed the position of the balls, carefully calculated the distance in such a manner that when she put one ball into the hole, the other would be at the right position for the next shot. Just as she planned, after one ball went into the hole, the other rolled to the place where she could hit it and put another ball into the hole.

That reminds me of a Vietnamese saying, "We cannot attain our goal if we hurry." A wise American teaches, "Easy does it." The Lord Jesus many times stated, "My time has not come." He patiently waited for His time, just like the sun.

Only the Gospel according to John recorded the story of Lazarus, one of the Lord's closest friends. When Lazarus was very sick, his sisters sent word to the Lord, "Lord, the one you love is sick." *"Yet when he heard that Lazarus was sick, he stayed where he was two more days"* (John 11:6). See how calm He was! Norman V. Peale called it "easy power." The Lord must have a lot of inner strength to stay calm in case of emergency. Today, when people want something, they want it right now. So, the sellers must put into the market instant products, from instant noodles to "microwaveable" dinners.

It had been four days when the Lord Jesus came to Bethany, Lazarus' hometown. However, with "easy power" Jesus raised His friend from the dead.

Power of the Water

Every day my wife and I try to walk for forty-five minutes to keep us in good shape, as Health Experts suggested. We walk along a wooded trail. The tall pine trees sometimes amaze us. The branches at the bottom are longer than the ones on the top of the trees. They are intelligently designed so that the trees can stand tall and firm. The roots suck the nutrients from the ground to feed the whole trunk and branches in such a way that no part is left behind.

The trees belong to the evergreen family. Whether it's raining or shining, whether it's snowing or freezing, the trees are always green. It takes a lot of power to make them grow. Who would say the trees evolved from seaweed?

Our physicians suggest that we should drink from six to eight glasses of water a day in addition to the 75% of water in the food we eat. Too often we forget to thank the Lord for His provision. People living in the cities rely on the City Utilities for water. When they receive a bill, some just pay the bill and forget about it for a month, some others complain that the bill is too high.

People living in the country have to dig their own wells. Either living in the cities or in the country, most people do not thank the Provider of the water, although we cannot survive without it. He distills the salt water, He uses clouds as trucks to carry millions of tons of water into the land, and changes vapor into drops of water so that they can fall down to the ground.

We just returned from our trip to Vietnam where the rain has been overdue for many months. In many areas, creeks and wells have dried out. Trees and livestock were dying. Low water levels have caused a shortage of hydroelectricity and the closing of industries that depend on electricity. Still, ninety-nine percent of the people didn't know that the Lord could make the rain fall down on their land.

Let's pause for a moment, and review the story of the Israelites. Approximately two million people were wandering in the desert in forty years. How could they survive if the Lord did not feed them with manna and give them water? How much manna, how much water did they need? God was able to supply all their needs.

The Book of Genesis described how the Lord created things in heaven and on the earth. He said, "Let there be . . ." and it came to pass as He said. He created things with the easy power of His word. The universe was created in six days. The narrative does not tell us how much power God has, but surely our finite mind cannot imagine.

"God is the source of all energy—energy in the universe, atomic energy, electrical energy, and spiritual energy; indeed every form of energy derives from the Creator." The Bible emphasizes this point when it says, *"He gives power to the faint; and to them that have no might he increases strength"* (Isaiah 40:29). [8]

The Power of the Word

God created every thing by the power of His word. He empowers His servants to speak the word and things happen as they speak.

Second Kings 1 recorded the story of the prophet Elijah who stopped King Ahaziah from consulting Baal-Zebub. The king sent to Elijah a captain with a company of fifty men. The captain went up to Elijah, and ordered the prophet to come down from the top of a hill. At this, Elijah answered the captain, *"If I am a man of God, may fire come down from heaven and consume you and your fifty men!" "Then fire fell from heaven and consumed the captain and his men"* (2 Kings 1:10).

The king then sent to Elijah another captain with his fifty men. Again Elijah called down the fire from Heaven to consume this company.

The second chapter of the same Book told us how Elisha inherited his teacher's office of prophet. After performing miracles Elisha went up to Bethel. The Bible tells us that some youths came out of the town and jeered at him, "Go on up, you bald-head!" Elisha's reaction was to call down a curse, and two bears came out of the wood and mauled forty-two of the youths.

The above stories indicate that the word of the prophet has power. A prophet is the one who tells forth, rather than foretells, even he can predict an event.

We read in the Book of Genesis that Esau and Jacob were fighting for their father's blessing, because the word of Isaac would eventually come to pass.

The diplomats can use their tongue to talk peace, and in some cases can spare the lives of thousand of people. On the contrary, the king can provoke another king with words that lead to war, and war leads to casualties.

Elisha spoke a word, and fifty-one men were destroyed in a second.

Years ago neurologists discovered that the language center of the brain is the headquarters controlling the whole nervous system. However, almost two thousand years ago, the apostle James had already taught that the tongue is a small member of our body, but has much power.

The language center of the brain has so much power over the whole body that a person can use the word to order his body to do what he wishes. For example, if a person continually says, "I feel weaker every day," immediately his nervous system receives that command, and it obeys, "I will weaken the body since the headquarters has commanded."

My eighty-five year old father-in-law went through two colon surgeries. Some days he felt better than the others. Sometimes he needed to go places, or to see his doctor, but his children were all busy. So he felt they failed to take care of him. When he didn't feel well, he prayed that the Lord take him home.

When we got together for a Bible study, I tried to lift him up, and gave him some encouragement. I suggested that he should recite Bible verses that build him up. I encouraged him to tell his body to be well, and to put himself in God's hand. When he started to have faith, to think good health, he felt better.

If a person says, "Oh, I can't do this," his nerves will respond promptly to that statement "Since the nervous control center told us that we can't, let's stop trying."

One of my former students is working for Lockheed Company as a machinist. He has known many who had retired from the Company, and died not long after their retirement. We may say that their bodies stopped working because their brain had decided to retire from life too.

The Bible had been written in a period of fifteen hundred years, and its last book, Revelation, was finished around 100 a.d. So, many think the Bible is no longer relevant to today's culture, and people need a better philosophy or a better worldview. The Bible is inerrant and infallible, and can provide us with truths that are helpful to enjoy a good life on earth. We don't need to feel bad. The language center in our brain can help us a great deal, if we believe God, and know how to use our tongue wisely.

The Bible teaches that, if we can control our tongue, we can take hold of our body. If so, why not use our tongue to bless others? Why don't we say the words of success and good health to ourselves and to our neighbors? Why don't we join the apostle Paul to affirm, *"I can do all things through Christ who strengthens me."*

There is a strange contradiction among my Vietnamese communities. People are not comfortable when talking about death. People do not wish anyone to know that they have a terminal illness. However, they use the word "death" so often in their daily conversation. We often hear the expressions like these: "tired to death," "hot to death," or "I suffer to death."

Indeed the Bible is still relevant. Today, all need to read the Bible to live a good life and to be ready when the Lord calls him home. It is the Book of hope that no other books can offer. The power of the word not only can help us to live a victorious life, but the Holy Spirit also wants us to use it to fulfill God's purpose.

We may have heard, or we may have seen "the workers of miracles" who just raised their hands, and people fell down, and received healing. I've always wondered about that. "Is that real?" I have asked myself. I would not say that they are false prophets.

In the Epistles written to the Romans, the Corinthians, and the Ephesians, Paul listed twenty-three gifts of the Holy Spirit. In I Corinthians 12, Paul states that the Holy Spirit gives to each of the believers just as He determines.

I know that the Holy Spirit has given me a couple of gifts, but they do not include the gift of healing. Sometimes I prayed for people, and they were healed. I was encouraged to pray more for many more people. I was asking the Lord for the gift of healing. He told me, though not with an audible voice, that the gift is given to me at my moment of need. I cannot own it, or keep it in my pocket. Twenty-three gifts listed in the Epistles of Paul, and all other gifts belong to God. They are available to all of His children. Whenever we need a gift, we just ask for it. We don't need to have a separate storage for the gifts.

The difference between a miracle worker and a Christian is the first knows how to ask the Lord for the power, and to exercise the power of the word, and to speak forth healing.

In Second Kings 5 we read the story of Naaman, the Commander of the king of Aram. The Bible says he was a valiant soldier, but he had leprosy. Fortunately, a young slave from Israel told him about the prophet Elisha who would cure him of his leprosy. So he went to see the king who urged him to go to Israel.

When Naaman stopped at the door of Elisha's house, he

expected a formal welcome. He had thought that the man of God would offer a religious sacrifice, and he would go through some sort of ritual. That is what magicians and sorcerers would do for Naaman. He was very angry when Elisha sent a messenger to say to him, "*Go, wash yourself seven times in the Jordan, and your flesh will be restored and you will be cleansed*" (2 Kings 5:10).

A true man of God speaks the word of God. When we hear God's word we have two choices: obey or disobey. Naaman believed Elisha could cure him of leprosy, but he did not completely trust the man of God. Fortunately, he had under him wise servants who gave him good advice. And Naaman was wise to listen to them, and became cleaned.

Second Kings 9 described how Jehu son of Jehoshaphat was anointed king over Israel. Jehu was in a staff meeting when a young prophet who was sent by Elisha came and asked to talk privately to him. When they were in the house alone "Then the prophet poured the oil on Jehu's head and declared, '*This is what the LORD, the God of Israel, says: I anoint you king over the LORD's people Israel. You are to destroy the house of Ahab your master, and I will avenge the blood of my servants the prophets and the blood of all the LORD's servants shed by Jezebel*'" (2 Kings 9:6–8).

It came to pass just as the Lord spoke through His servant. "*When Jehu came to Samaria, he killed all who were left there of Ahab's family; he destroyed them, according to the word of the LORD spoken to Elijah*" (2 Kings 10:17).

A very well known Pastor of a Korean Church shared his experience, "The Lord spoke to me, 'you may feel the strong presence of the Holy Spirit in your Church, but nothing has happened, no soul has been saved, no broken home restored until you speak out. Give me foundation to do wonders.' " Yes Lord," the Pastor answered, "I'm sorry to grieve you. I'm going to speak out." He was not at ease; he didn't know what people would think about him. So he told the Lord, "Lord, I'm afraid, I will not command the lame to get up, nor cancer to disappear. I will start with the headache instead."

Later, during a Church service, even he could see in the spirit the lame walking, the tumors vanishing, he ignored them. He only said, "Someone is healed of the headache." Immediately one person was healed. He was shaken when he saw things coming to pass at a simple word.

Let's study a couple of cases of healing performed by the Lord Jesus himself.

"*Some men brought to him a paralytic, lying on a mat. When Jesus saw their faith, he said to the paralytic, 'Take heart, son; your sins are forgiven'*" (Matthew 9:2). First, the Lord spoke forth the word of forgiveness, since that was a prerequisite for the healing of the paralytic. Next, He said the healing words "*Get up and walk.*" It came to pass as He had spoken.

Another interesting story was that of a woman who had lived a sinful life. She had learned that the Lord was invited to Simon's home for dinner. She also came to the party, but not to partake of the meal because she was not invited. She was there just to show her repentance and her worship by wiping the Lord's feet, by kissing them, and by pouring perfume on them. "*Then Jesus said to her, 'Your sins are forgiven'*" (Luke 7:48). He spoke the word of forgiveness to the woman. We know that she is now with Him in Paradise for eternity.

The Bible is the very word of God. It has the power to heal, to deliver people from sins and from various kinds of troubles. That is the reason why the Bible is the best seller. It has an eternal value as the Lord Jesus asserts, "*Heaven and earth will pass away, but my words will never pass away*" (Matthew 24:35). When we speak out what we believe, it will come to pass. An illustration of that statement is found in Luke 13. A woman, who had been crippled by a spirit for eighteen years, was in one of the synagogues where the Lord Jesus taught. The Lord said to her, *"Woman, you are set free from your infirmity."* Then he put his hands on her, *"and immediately she straightened up and praised God"* (Luke 13:13). The Lord spoke forth the word of healing; His word touched the woman and healed her.

In the Book of Acts we see another illustration of the power of the word. Acts 3 relates the healing of a crippled man at the temple gate called Beautiful. Of course, it's a beautiful story. The crippled beggar looked ugly to the worshippers, but beautiful in God's sight. God healed the man so he could look good to men. The miracle was beautiful. Peter and John did not have anything to offer to the crippled, *"Silver and gold I do not have,"* Peter said to the man. What the apostles had was God's healing power. They could access the power to heal the beggar "at three in the afternoon," and at the temple gate because they "had been with Jesus." They just spoke the word in Jesus' Name, and the sick man was healed.

The key word is "had been with Jesus." The power comes from abiding in Him, never losing sight of Him. He promises to all believers, *"I am the vine; you are the branches. If a man remains in me and I in him, he will bear much fruit; apart from me you can do nothing"* (John 15:5–6).

Sometime, without knowing, we might say something that could damage the self-image of someone. If we tell a child that he doesn't amount to much, or he can do nothing good, and if that child believes that lie, he will be as we say to him.

In the Book of Genesis we find an illustration of the above fact. We know that Esau sold his birth right for a bowl of soup. However, he wanted his father's blessing so much that he wished to kill his brother Jacob, after his brother received the blessing his father had promised him.

Power in the Blood

After God put Adam in the Garden of Eden, He commanded the man, *"You are free to eat from any tree in the garden; but you must not eat from the tree of the knowledge of good and evil, for when you eat of it you will surely die"* (Genesis 2:16b, 17). The Lord was so gracious to Adam when He allowed the man to do ninety-nine things, and only reserved one thing for Himself. Adam, who was blessed with a close relationship with the Creator, understood exactly how serious the Lord was. But the man failed to obey his Master, and ate of the tree of knowledge of good and evil.

God's judgment must be executed. However, by His grace, the Lord sacrificed an animal to atone for Adam and Eve. From that moment animals must be sacrificed for the remission of sin. Cain and Abel, Adam's two sons, offered sacrifices to the Lord. Cain offered some of the fruits of the soil, while Abel brought fat portions from some of the first born of his flock. The Lord did not look with favor on Cain and his offering because the fruits of the soil did not meet the requirements for sin offerings.

From that point of time, apparently mankind became more and more wicked. The Bible tells us, *"The LORD was grieved that he had made man on the earth, and his heart was filled with pain."* He had no other choices but to wipe out *"everything on dry land that had the breath of life in its nostrils"* (Genesis 7:22), except for Noah and his family. Genesis 8 describes how Noah expressed his thanksgiving unto the Lord. The wise man says, "First thing first," and Noah knew what should be his first priority. There were many urgent tasks to do, but the man was mindful of God, his Deliverer. He began to build an altar, and sacrificed burnt offerings on it. While Abraham is the ancestor of the line of Shem, Noah is the ancestor of all mankind. I'd give him credit for setting a beautiful example for all human beings living on the earth.

Unfortunately not all his children followed his example. Slowly they moved away from the Deliverer of their fathers. The city of Babel and its tower were the signs of their separation from the Lord. The city was built to glorify and fortify themselves, and the tower, to worship the sun, the moon, and the stars, instead of the Creator. God had to draw their attention to the real purpose of their lives. This time He decided to disperse them so they could multiply and fill the earth.

In approximately 2000 b.c. God initiated a plan of salvation with a man of faith, Abram. God's covenant with Abram revealed the promise of a Messiah, "and all peoples on earth will be blessed through you" (Genesis 12:3b). The Lord also promised to Abram "a great nation." From the line of Abram, Jacob was chosen to carry out the messianic promise. But, at one point, the chosen family faced the danger of being wiped out by a severe drought in the land. No natural disaster could harm the chosen family. God allowed Jacob and his family to move and stay in Egypt for four hundred years, and to prepare them for the important event. After four hundred years the Israelites increased in number. It was time for them to move into the Promised Land.

The night they exited Egypt God established a very significant ceremony, the Passover that they must observe yearly. The key element of the Feast was the Passover Lamb. Each household was to kill a lamb. "The blood was to be sprinkled 'on side and lintel, where it might be looked to, not on the threshold to be trodden underfoot'" (Jamieson, Fausset, and Brown). By this act both the house and those dwelling in it were to be expiated (by the use of blood and hyssop; cf. Lev 14:4–7; Num 19:1 ff.) and consecrated unto God. [9] The lamb was sacrificed to set apart the nation of Israel to be a "Nation under God." As they traveled, God guided them in a pillar of cloud by day, and in a pillar of fire by night.

Through Moses the Lord issued the Ten Commandments, and the Mosaic laws. God's Law must be followed, but He knows that no one is able to strictly follow His Law. Thus, He provided His people with atonement through animal sacrifices. However, that was a temporary solution for Christ's true atonement, once and for all on the cross.

"The blood of goats and bulls and the ashes of a heifer sprinkled on those who are ceremonially unclean sanctify them so that they are outwardly clean. How much more, then, will the blood of Christ, who through the eternal Spirit offered himself unblemished to God, cleanse our consciences from acts that lead to death, so that we may serve the living God" (Hebrews 9:13–14). Throughout the Old Testament, from the time God Himself made atonement for Adam, the shedding of blood has been required for remission of sin. Sin is always a wall separating sinners to the Holy One. God always wishes to draw close to human beings because He loves them. But the blood of goats and bulls were only temporary, pending Christ's permanent sacrifice. There is real power in the blood. Christ's blood gives Him power over death. His blood gives us power over sin, and death. Without His blood we are still under the laws of sin and death.

Rhema versus Logos

English uses "word" to translate two Greek terms *"logos"* and *"rhema."*

The Bible says that God spoke and things were. He created the universe by His *logos*. When we read the Bible or God's word from Genesis to Revelation, we receive the knowledge of God and of His promises. However, knowing and understanding God will not give us faith. In Romans 10:17, *"Consequently, faith comes from hearing the message, and the message is heard through the word of Christ;"* the message or word correlates to the Greek word *"rhema."*

One scholar defines *logos* as *"the said word of God,"* and *rhema* as *"the saying word of God."* Thayer's Greek Lexicon defines rhema as:
1) Properly, that which is or has been uttered by the living voice, thing spoken, word;
2) In imitation of the Hebrew "daabaar," the subject matter of speech, thing spoken of, thing.

Pastor Yonggi Cho defines *rhema* as "a special word for a special person in a special situation." For illustration purposes Pastor Cho told the story of three Korean young ladies who drowned when they tried to walk on the water. He said that those girls practiced their faith based on the word of God. However, the Lord didn't have any reasons to support their faith. The difference between Peter and those young Koreans was the Lord Jesus spoke to Peter. He heard the *rhema* of his Master, *"Come."*

"Many think they believe God's word," Cho said, "but they can't differentiate between the word that brings knowledge of God and the word that conveys faith in a special situation of the human heart. This kind of faith triggers miracles."

Both Matthew and Luke recorded the "Temptation of Jesus" in the wilderness. Both Eve and Jesus were tempted by the devil. Both had the knowledge of the word of God. But while Eve used *logos*, our Lord used *rhema* in dealing with the tempter.

When we read the Bible we read the word written by the writers of the Bible. That word does not have any effect on our hearts until we meet the Lord through His word; only then the *rhema* has the power to change us, to heal us. In other words, *logos* becomes *rhema* when the Lord speaks to us through His word.

Through the prophet Hosea the Lord explains to the Israelites the reason why they perish, *"My people are destroyed from lack of knowledge. Because you have rejected knowledge, I also reject you as my priests; because you have ignored the law of your God, I also will ignore your children"* (Hosea 4:6).

They may know the *logos*, not the *rhema*. That is why they are destroyed. Through the *rhema* we know God's will.

Last week, a Pastor who is leaving a local Vietnamese Church called me and asked whether I'd be willing to take over the leadership of that Church. "I need to pray about that," I replied. "I believe I'm called to stand in the gap, rather than to be a Senior Pastor. If the church board would like me to be the Pastor, I wish to meet with them."

"OK," the Pastor answered, "I will arrange a meeting for us."

And I prayed, and I waited, and I waited until Monday of this week, but he did not call me back.

Then, I asked the Lord, "What has happened? Do you want to open the door for me?" "KH," the Lord answered.

The letter K is pronounced CA that sounds like "car" meaning sing, in Vietnamese. The letter H is pronounced HAT that also means sing. The Lord wants me to praise Him when I wait on Him for an answer.

"Our Father which art in heaven, Hallowed be thy name."

Next time, God told me, "KHO" which means dry. I said, "Yes, Lord I'm dry. I need a new anointing, rain down on me. I'm thirsty, would you come and fill me now."

Then, He says, "KHON" which means wise. I said, "I got it now. I read your *logos*, but I need your *rhema* to be wise, and to know your will."

Then He gives me the final answer "KHONG' which means NO. "Yes, Lord."

"Thy will be done on earth, as it is in heaven."

His thoughts are higher than my thoughts; His way is higher than my way. I'm happy with His decision.

I believe Father God loves to surprise His children just like a natural father because He wants to have fun with us. As soon as I was satisfied with His decision I received an email from one of the missionaries in Cambodia. She asked me to do some translation for her. She is ministering to the Vietnamese, and needs some English books translated into Vietnamese. Praise the Lord!

Last month my wife and I had a chance to meet with a man for the first time. We had learned that he was not doing well. We wished to share with him the Good News of the Lord Jesus. I started to suggest that he should belong to a faith community, preferably a Christian Church. He told me that he was baptized in a Mormon church, and had studied the Bible for some time. He thinks Mormons are nice people, and Mormonism is a good religion.

However, after the memorable event on September 11, 2001 he lost his faith in God and in the Bible. He stated that there is no God, and the Bible is not the truth. To him, if there were God, He would not have let a terrible thing like that happen. "Where is God?" He asked.

Now I understand why he lost his faith in God. That is because he gained head knowledge or *logos,* but not *rhema,* or the heart knowledge.

Based on the teaching of the apostle Paul in his Epistle to the Ephesians, the problem with this man was that Christ has never dwelt in his heart, and that he has never been rooted and grounded in love. When one believer does not have a personal relationship with Jesus Christ, when he does not acknowledge Him as Lord and Savior, he is not born again. It will not be difficult for such person to abandon his faith.

In his book "Priority Of Knowing God" Peter V. Deison tells

the story of Ramad, an Indian, who used to be a gang member. One time he broke in a house; he saw on a table a black book with pages made from thin papers, good for homemade cigarettes. [10] He took the book, and every day he tore one page to make cigarettes. When he tore one page he would read the writing on that page.

One night, after he had read a page, he knelt down, repented of his sin, and asked the Lord Jesus to save him. And he decided to turn himself in, and the police were so amazed. He spent time in prison, was changed into a good man, and led many to the Lord.

God's word became Living word to Ramad when he met the Lord, and the power of the Gospel transformed him.

"Religion can reform but only the Gospel can transform." (Peter V. Deison)

Where Do We Get Our Power?

"*Now to him who is able to do immeasurably more than all we ask or imagine, according to his power that is at work within us, to him be glory in the church and in Christ Jesus throughout all generations, for ever and ever! Amen*" (Ephesians 3:20).

What is required of us is faith as big as a mustard seed. But, sometimes we do not have enough faith to believe that God is able to do more than all we ask or imagine. It is encouraging to know that His power is at work within us. We need to believe and release that power to our physical strength and to that of others.

Samson was a mighty man of God. He was a superman of his time. Where did all his might come from? Apparently not from his long hairs, but when "*The Spirit of the LORD came upon him in power*" (Judges 14:6, 19; 15:14—NIV).

That's right, the key words are "the Spirit of the Lord." Human beings are only statues or robots if the Lord does not breathe into our nostrils the breath of life.

Zechariah, born in Babylon, was a prophet and priest. He prophesied for a period of three years. His message was not "doom and gloom," but "glorious future."

By 520 b.c. Israel was reduced to an insignificant number. Zechariah tried to let God's people know that the situation was only temporary, and one day their Messiah will come, and they would again be a great nation. Zechariah was the prophet of restoration and glory. He did not condemn, but rather revealed the presence of the Lord through many glorious descriptive stories that edified them. Particularly Zechariah encouraged Zerubbabel who was aware of his limitations, *"Not by might nor by power, but by my Spirit,' says the LORD Almighty"* (Zechariah 4:6—NIV).

It is very true; no one can do anything by his own strength. But we can do all things through Christ who provides us with His mighty power. He has overcome the world; we can conquer sins that hinder us from enjoying an abundant life in Christ Jesus.

The Fruits of the Spirit Give Us Power

Love

Second Samuel 23 lists David's mighty men. At that time David was at the cave of Adullam, in the stronghold, while the Philistine garrison was at Bethlehem. David wished that someone would get him some water. Three mighty men knew there was a well near the gate of Bethlehem. They broke through the Philistine lines, drew the water from the well, and carried it back to David. But he refused to drink the water because they risked their lives to get him a drink.

The three mighty men chose to follow David because they loved him. David could not make them follow him, nor go to Bethlehem to draw water from the well. They did that out of love. When David had the water he had longed for, he refused to drink it because he knew that was not right for him to ask them to risk their lives just for a drink.

Love must be the main motivation for all of our actions, *"Do nothing out of selfish ambition or vain conceit, but in humility consider others better than yourselves. Each of you should look not only to your own interests, but also to the interests of others"* (Philippians 2:3–4—NIV).

While the world has a hard time looking after the interests of others, true followers of Christ, by His power, can deny themselves for the interests of others. It takes a lot of energy to love.

While I'm writing these lines, Ms. Condolezza Rice, the US Secretary of State, is visiting a refugee camp in Sudan. The television showed her talking to the children and women of that country. She is there, representing a world-leading country, but her message is not, "I am a powerful lady, I am holding a key position in a great nation, you have to respect me." Her mission is to find ways to help a country in need where, for over two years, conflict has torn apart the lives of over 2.5 million people, mostly women and children. The children of Sudan are threatened by measles, polio, and hunger. Rice is bringing the true love of the United States to Sudan. That is the true power, the power of love. The apostle whom Jesus loves asserts, "God is love." Whoever loves has God in him, and has the power of the Almighty God.

Through the Bible, God reveals Himself as a loving God. He loves us unconditionally. When He loves us, He does not ask for anything back. Moses wrote, *"The LORD, the LORD, the compassionate and gracious God, slow to anger, abounding in love and faithfulness"* (Ex 34:6). The phrase "abounding in love" is repeated in Numbers (14:18), in Nehemiah (9:17), in Psalms (86:15; 103:8), in Joel (3:13), and in Jonah (4:2).

Joy

"Do not grieve, for the joy of the LORD is your strength" (Nehemiah 8:10).

God as the Bible reveals to us is personal, while other religions do not present the Lord as such. He is personal, so his relationship to His people means a lot to Him. The fact that God visited Adam in the Garden of Eden indicates that He creates people so that He can enjoy them.

When the Lord says, *"You shall have no other gods before me"* (Exodus 20:3), He wants His people know that they belong to Him, and to Him alone. He definitely does not want to see any third party between Him and His people, for *"I, the Lord your God, am a jealous God"* (Exodus 20:5). The Old Testament compares His relationship to His people to that of a husband and his wife. That means he wants His people to keep an intimate relationship with Him.

Of course, any relationship has conflicts. The Old Testament shows that God did not always have great time with His people. God's chosen people were called to love Him with all their heart, all their soul, and all their strength. Unfortunately, too often they did not meet His expectation, so He had to punish them because He was just.

Time and time again God's people turned away from Him. They failed Him miserably. God had delivered Israel from Egypt in about 1446 b.c. Over seven hundred years later the people of the Northern Kingdom was taken into captivity to Babylon. In 586 b.c. the Babylonians also carried the Southern Kingdom's people into exile.

However, seventy years later the Lord used Cyrus, king of Persia to allow His people to return to their land. The first time, Zerubbabel led fifty thousand Jews. Nehemiah returned about sixty-five years after Zerubbabel.

Immediately after coming to Jerusalem, Nehemiah secretly inspected the damage. Then he called together the leaders of Israel and revealed his plan to rebuild the walls and the gates of Jerusalem. The undertaking was not without opposition, not only from the enemies, but also from within their own ranks.

Finally, the walls were finished in spite of crafty opposition. God's people had reason to celebrate. On that occasion the Law of Moses was read from morning until noon. Many were overcome with emotion, as they had never before heard the Word of God. They wept, but Nehemiah urged the people to rejoice because "the joy of the Lord is (their) strength."

Approximately five hundred years later Paul wrote his letter to the Philippians. It seemed strange that someone can advise free people to rejoice when he was imprisoned in Rome. Joy was the key thought of his epistle. Joy and related emotions occur nineteen times in Philippians. Joy is a fruit of the Holy Spirit, and it does not depend on circumstances. That kind of joy comes only from a close relationship with the Lord. In Him we can have joy. He gives us the power to enjoy even in trials and tribulation. That was why Paul could sincerely say, "*I rejoice greatly in the Lord that at last you have renewed your concern for me*" (Philippians 4:10), and he could urge the Philippians, "*Rejoice in the Lord always. I will say it again: Rejoice*" (4:4).

The apostle Peter tells us not to get bogged down by all kinds of trials because they are temporary. But we should rejoice instead, because our faith will be greater after being tested. He also tells us to rejoice so that we can participate in the sufferings of Christ, so that we may be overjoyed when his glory is revealed (I Peter 4:13).

The apostle James says "Amen" to the other two in stating, "*Consider it pure joy, my brothers, whenever you face trials of many kinds, because you know that the testing of your faith develops perse-*

verance. *Perseverance must finish its work so that you may be mature and complete, not lacking anything*" (James 1:2–5).

Were the apostles sorry for themselves, they would lose all their strength because they could not see the Lord was on their side. Their close relationship with the Lord Jesus gave them the power to enjoy abundant life in Christ Jesus. Christians need to learn how to rejoice in hostile situations because there are more bumpy roads than smooth highways. As the Lord has warned us, "*I have told you these things, so that in me you may have peace. In this world you will have trouble. But take heart! I have overcome the world*" (John 16:33).

Peace

Many things in life can contribute to our misery: anxiety, worries, fear, hate, conflicts, jealousy, fighting, and so on. People try to have peace, peace within their family, with their neighbors, with their co-workers. Many are religious, and all religions, except for Satan's religion, teach their followers to live in peace with everybody.

It is sad to say that since the "fall of man" there has been no peace. The first son of the first man Adam killed his younger brother Abel, just because he did not present the right offering to the Lord. Ever since, humankind has been restless. That is because sin has entered into the world, and all have sinned and come short of the glory of God. Sin and its ramifications are sure to take away our peace.

Peace matters much to the world and to all of us. But, if the Lord Jesus does not reign in our hearts we will never have peace. Man cannot have peace if he is not at peace with God. And peace with God can only be obtained through the death of Jesus Christ. One can only draw near to God by Jesus' reconciliation. The world and its religious systems do not provide that kind of peace.

They try different ways of bringing peace to themselves, to feel good. Some have taught that one may do whatever makes them feel good, regardless of the moral values. They contradict themselves by saying to do good to our neighbors, and to do whatever makes us feel good, even that which can hurt our neighbors. Christians, on the other hand, may do whatever pleases God and our neighbors.

The Lord Jesus is the Prince of Peace. Through Him we have peace with God and with man. Through Him we can be in harmony with God, and have the power to live an abundant life as He intends for us to live.

Our Power Resides in the Word of God

God is almighty. His word is also powerful. He speaks and things come to pass, *"By the word of the LORD were the heavens made, their starry host by the breath of his mouth"* (Psalm 33:6). Some say that the Bible is two to three thousand years old, and it is no longer relevant to the culture of the 21st century. That is not the case, as history has shown. The word of God is inerrant and infallible, *"So shall My word be that goes forth from My mouth; it shall not return to Me void, but it shall accomplish what I please, and it shall prosper in the thing for which I sent it"* (Isaiah 55:11—NKJV).

The authority of the word of God is the same yesterday, today and forever. It will never lose its power.

The Lord Jesus uses the word of God to settle any argument with His enemies. The Lord Jesus implies that His words are equal to God's word when He asserts, *"Heaven and earth will pass away, but my words will never pass away"* (Matthew 24:35).

With such authority and power how can God's word and the Gospel of our Lord Jesus make a difference in our life? We need to open the book of Joshua to learn the Lord's instruction to this man.

After the death of Moses, God gave to Joshua the responsibility of leading His people into the Promised Land. He did not say to the new commander, "Joshua, you will succeed Moses, my servant, as the leader of my people. I will sit down with you, and teach you all you need to know to win the war and how to occupy the land." But, rather God was more concerned about Joshua knowing His word. In a matter of fact, God commanded Joshua to pay close attention to His word, *"This Book of the Law shall not depart from your mouth, but you shall meditate in it day and night, that you may observe to do according to all that is written in it. For then you will make your way prosperous, and then you will have good success"* (Joshua 1:8—NKJV).

The Lord gave Joshua the keys to prosperity and success. They were: to read His word, to speak His word, to share His word, to meditate on His word, and to obey His word. How was Joshua doing? He claimed before God's people that he and his family would serve the Lord. He was successful because he obeyed God. Today, if we want to be successful and prosperous we can follow Joshua's example.

The Bible has no power if we read it in the wrong way or for the wrong reason. We need to read the word of God with the desire to be transformed, and it will do us good. To meditate in the Scripture means to allow it to penetrate the depth of our heart, and then hide it like we would hide a treasure, so that no one can have his hand on it.

Toward the end of his life, Moses took time to teach the Israelites valuable lessons. He presented them the conditions of God's blessings and the reason of His cursing. Blessings shall come upon those who diligently obey the voice of the LORD God, and who observe carefully all His commandments which

Moses command them at that time (Deuteronomy 28:1). And cursed are those who do not obey the voice of the LORD, and do not observe carefully all His commandments and His statutes as Moses commanded them.

Many people have testified that the word of God has touched them, healed them, and transformed them. When we feel depressed, when we feel lonesome, God's word can lift us up, and strengthen us.

If we feel weak, Isaiah 40:31 has the power to restore our strength,

> *"But those who wait on the LORD*
> *Shall renew their strength;*
> *They shall mount up with wings like eagles,*
> *They shall run and not be weary,*
> *They shall walk and not faint."*

When the Lord asks us to do something, and we do not feel confident in our ability, Philippians 4:13 will give us some encouragement, *"I can do all things through Christ who strengthens me."*

The reading of the Bible will not do us well until it sinks deep into our subconscious, and until it becomes our guide.

According to the Lord Jesus, the Holy Spirit is our Counselor. How does He counsel God's people? The Holy Spirit cannot speak out loud, but He can direct our mind to the right Scripture.

6

The Power of the Crowd

The Tent of Meeting and temple were meeting places of the people with the Lord.

Speaking to the Samaritan woman, the Lord Jesus made known to us that we are no longer required to worship God either in Jerusalem or on the Mount of Gerizim. Christians may worship in any church that worships in spirit and in truth. We may even worship God in our own room, in front of a TV, watching an anointed man of God preaching. However, the crowd, the gathering of God's people put more weight on the petition submitted to Him. Has He required two people to agree on anything before He grants our request (Matthew 18:19)? A Vietnamese maxim states, "One tree cannot make a hill, three trees together will make a mountain."

On the day called "Palm Sunday" the Lord came into Jerusalem to celebrate the Passover. He was welcomed as a king. Matthew 21 described:

> "*A very large crowd spread their cloaks on the road, while others cut branches from the trees and spread them on the road. The crowds that went ahead of him and those that followed shouted, 'Hosanna to the Son of David! Blessed is he who comes in the name of the Lord!' 'Hosanna in the highest!' When Jesus entered Jerusalem, the whole city was stirred and asked, 'Who is this?'"*
>
> (Matthew 21:8–10)

If the Lord Jesus was a human leader like the Maccabees, He would have stirred up the crowd, and said, "Men of Abraham, Isaac, and Jacob, follow me, we will expel the Romans out of our City."

But, just four days later, the same crowd which had shouted *"Hosanna to the Son of David! Blessed is he who comes in the name of the Lord,"* now demanded, *"Crucify him!"* They did not represent the majority, they were just a small group, but, by joining together, they were able to send the Lord to the cross.

A ball of snow becomes bigger and bigger by rolling and picking up more snow. A small ball of snow melts down in a shorter period of time than a bigger ball of snow.

The author of the Book of Hebrews urged Christians to draw near to God, and not to forget to meet together as often as they could. As Christians assemble to worship, the bigger the number, the more power they can receive to do God's will. The writer of the Book of Hebrews wrote, *"Let us not give up meeting together, as some are in the habit of doing, but let us encourage one another-and all the more as you see the Day approaching"* (Hebrews 10:25).

The Book of Matthew recorded the last hour our Lord spent with His loved ones in the garden of Gethsemane. That was a very tense moment when our Lord felt sorrowful and troubled. He said, *"My soul is overwhelmed with sorrow to the point of death.*

Stay here and keep watch with me" (Matthew 26:38). We understand why He took His inner circle to that place of retreat. At that very moment He desperately needed their presence and spiritual support. But, apparently none of His chosen understood what taking place in the depth of His soul. They were physically tired. Even the Lord Jesus did not want to struggle alone; we too do not need to fight alone in our daily struggle. The meeting together with our brothers and sisters and their corporate power are our best weapons.

As a Vietnamese saying goes, "We are darkened when we are close to the ink, but we are brightened when we get closer to the light." There is one similar idea in the Book of Proverbs, "*He who walks with the wise grows wise, but a companion of fools suffers harm*" (Proverbs 13:20). The spiritual application of those teachings is that Christians should regularly have fellowship with other believers if they want to grow. Many churches now start to see the benefits of small groups.

My wife and I were born again in a small country church of less than fifty members. We attended that Church for seventeen years, and we love the people. They were like our relatives.

Then it was time for us to move on to a bigger church of five hundred members. At the new church, nobody knew us, and we didn't know anyone well. At first, we felt uncomfortable because we did not have a close relationship with anybody.

The pastors shook the hands of the long-time members of the church. They hugged each other very warmly, but they seemed distant to us. However, by God's grace we could keep up with that not so good feeling for a while.

Then I went to one retreat with a group of men. I got to know them, and they learned a little bit about me. After that first introduction, I went to the monthly Men's Breakfast, and we started to have a closer relationship.

Less than a year after we had attended the first service there, maybe thirty percent of the church was acquainted with my family. Actually, my daughter, her husband, and their two daughters had been attending that church for six months when we came.

One time my daughter experienced some tough times. We prayed fervently, and the Lord answered our prayers, healing her relationship through the wise counseling of the senior pastor.

We had advised our daughter and her husband to get involved in the church activities, such as small group Bible study. But they had been busy doing their own things, and they were not interested in the Church business.

Now, as they had experienced God's grace, they started to understand what Paul spoke about meeting together with other believers.

In the animal kingdom, the one that stays away from the herd is likely to be attacked by the predators. When the animals hang together in one mighty group, it is very tough for the predators to get them. Spiritually speaking, Christians who are prayed for, edified by other Christians can fight a good fight of faith, and come out victorious. In spite of his maturity, a lone Christian, who relies on himself can hardly stand the attack of the authorities and the powers of this dark world and of the spiritual forces of evil in the heavenly realms. The enemies can easily defeat a lone Christian.

Two weeks ago, I had a dream. I saw myself wandering in an open zoo, partly fenced. On my right, I saw tigers and lions; one tiger was fighting with a lion. I kept on walking when I saw some predators down the road. Then I realized that I'd better turn around, and to leave that place as quickly as possible if I didn't want to be a delicious dinner for those beasts.

As a matter of fact, it is a jungle out there as the apostle Peter already warned us, *"Be self-controlled and alert. Your enemy the devil prowls around like a roaring lion looking for someone to devour"* (1

Peter 5:8). To survive in a hostile environment one must stick to his pack.

Of course we do not need to attend church services on a regular basis to go to heaven. But church attendance and fellowship with believers do strengthen and help a believer to grow and to overcome troubles.

Human Weakness

The apostle Paul states, "*For when I am weak, then I am strong*" (2 Corinthians 12:10b). How can that be? We've learned in school that weak is the opposite of strong. How can a weak man be strong? So we cannot take Paul's assertion literally.

The attitude of the Lord Jesus described in Paul's epistle to the Philippians may help us to understand that antithesis. According to the Scripture, Christ Jesus is equal with God, but He made Himself nothing before He can be confessed as Lord.

> "*He humbled himself and became obedient to death—even death on a cross! Therefore God exalted him to the highest place and gave him the name that is above every name, that at the name of Jesus every knee should bow, in heaven and on earth and under the earth, and every tongue confess that Jesus Christ is Lord, to the glory of God the Father.*"
> (Philippians 2:8–11)

Based on Christ Jesus' example, we will be strong when we humble ourselves, and let Him direct our path. For His Name's sake the Lord Jesus will guide us in the paths of His righteousness. He will fill us with His overcoming power when we are willing to empty ourselves of our human strength, of our pride, of our wisdom.

Today, wherever the Gospel is preached, people know of Moses. And we know he was a great leader, a lawgiver, and a prophet. The Bible also told us that at the time of his birth the decree commanding the slaying of all male babies was in force. So Moses was considered as dead, but the Lord called him and set him apart to be part of His great plan for the Jewish people and for all Christians today.

We learn from the Book of Exodus that Moses was saved and adopted by the daughter of the man who had issued his death decree. As the adopted son of a princess, or grandson of the king, Moses received great education in the court of the most civilized nation of that time.

However, when the Lord called Moses to return to Egypt, and to deliver His people from the land of bondage, Moses responded that he was "slow of speech and slow of tongue." In other words, he said, "Look, Lord, your plan is so awesome, I like it very much, but Lord, I'm weak, I'm unable to carry out your plan. I'm sorry!"

We know that Moses was a sophisticated man. Maybe he was still feeling guilty, and forty years in the wilderness of Midian wore him down. He was not as confident as when he had been forty years old. The Lord knew that Moses was more than an able man and that he needed a word of encouragement. So the Lord promised, *"I will be with you."* What more did Moses need? And what more do we need to do anything, *"If God is for us, who can be against us?"* Moses could not have accomplished what he did if God had not been with him. It is also true with all God's children today. The apostle Paul agreed with that statement when he said, *"I can do all things through Christ who strengthens me."*

Through the Book of Exodus we have learned that Moses was a great leader. The Lord chose the right man for the job. He led God's people to the Promised Land. Even though he did not cross the Jordan River, he was actually in the Land. He finished well. Moses also wrote the Pentateuch, the first five Books of the Bible. They are important books of the Old Testament due to the fact that they are "the Bible in miniature" according to J. Sidlow Baxter. Genesis presents the ruin through the sin of man; Exodus, the redemption by blood; Leviticus, the communion on the ground of atonement; Numbers, the guidance by he will of God; and Deuteronomy, the destination through the faithfulness of God.[11]

First Kings 18 narrates how Elijah the prophet slaughtered four hundred and fifty prophets of Baal who were protected by the ungodly Queen Jezebel. It took a lot of courage to accomplish such an exploit. However, when Elijah learned that the Queen would take revenge for her prophets, he was afraid and ran for his life. When he came to Beersheba in Judah, he sat under a broom tree, and *"prayed that he might die. 'I have had enough, LORD,' he said. 'Take my life; I am no better than my ancestors'"* (1 Kings 19:4).

At that moment Elijah was at the bottom of the valley. But the Lord was not finished with him yet. After he strengthened the depressed prophet with bread and water, the Lord sent him on a new mission. Just like Moses, Elijah needed a pat on the back.

Like the man of God we all need to be reminded that we cannot rely on our own strength because we don't have much. But if we rely on the Lord's power, we can do many great things. Did our Lord Jesus say, *"I tell you the truth, anyone who has faith in me will do what I have been doing. He will do even greater things than these, because I am going to the Father"* (John 14:12)?

Sin Weakens Us

"For the wages of sin is death, but the gift of God is eternal life in Christ Jesus our Lord" (Romans 6:23).

We have the tendency to offer ourselves to someone to obey as slaves, whether we are slaves to sin, or to obedience. And we all know that slaves have no fun. They are at the mercy of their masters. They do what their masters command them to do, and most of the time against their will. Many slaves would flee from their masters to be free and to have a better life.

We all have to work, and the work of a slave will be harder. The labor of a slave weakens him, so sin weakens the one who is slave to sin.

Sin is already a sign of weakness. Spiritual maturity may stop a Christian from sinning. At the very moment a mature Christian thinks about an evil act the Holy Spirit within him waves a stop sign at him. If he is sensitive enough he will turn away from that thought, and he is delivered from sin. On the contrary, a carnal man keeps on thinking about the evil act because it entertains him well. The more he meditates on evil, the more he sinks deep into sin to the point he cannot escape, and he has no other choice than to surrender to sin which leads to death.

Is there any hope for an immature Christian? Yes, God has come down from heaven just to save the lost. The Bible teaches us, *"But where sin increased, grace increased all the more"* (Romans 5:20). If we were all spiritually strong, Jesus would not have had to die to free us from our sin. Repentance shows our weakness, but our strength will be restored, and we will be stronger. God will not despise the broken spirit and the contrite heart. He will bless the one who mourns, who really feels sorry for his sin.

The Apostle whom Jesus loves, has heard from the Lord, and declared, *"God is light, in Him there is no darkness at all"* (1 John

1:5). He goes on to say that we should walk in the light, as he is in the light. We will have fellowship with one another, and the blood of Jesus, God's Son, purifies us from all sin.

The apostle Paul teaches on the same subject, saying, *"For you were once darkness, but now you are light in the Lord. Live as children of light"* (Ephesians 5:8). *"The fruit of the light consists in all goodness, righteousness and truth"* (Ephesians 5:9). He wants His children to have those characteristics. On the other hand, if we walk in the dark, our deeds are fruitless. We will live as children of light when we will live wisely, for we will know what the Lord's will is. On the contrary, when we live as children of darkness, we will be foolish.

The world we live in can be divided into two parts: the kingdom of God and the kingdom of the darkness. The latter is, *"darkened in their understanding and separated from the life of God because of the ignorance that is in them due to the hardening of their hearts"* (Ephesians 4:18). In his epistle to the Romans, Paul asserts, *"The man without the Spirit does not accept the things that come from the Spirit of God, for they are foolishness to him, and he cannot understand them, because they are spiritually discerned"* (1 Corinthians 2:14).

A carnal man is an ignorant man because his heart is hardened. And for this reason, he is morally insensitive, and easily gives himself *"over to sensuality so as to indulge in every kind of impurity, with a continual lust for more"* (Ephesians 4:19).

8

The Armor of God

After World War Two, Russia rose to the position of the so-called Super Power that had the potential to conquer any European nation. In 1946 Stalin declared that peace was impossible "under the present capitalist development of the world economy." Winston Churchill delivered a dramatic speech in Fulton, Missouri, with President Truman sitting in the platform. Churchill declared that Britain and the United States had to work together to counter Soviet threat.

In 1949 thirteen countries signed a treaty called the North Atlantic Treaty Organization or NATO. The purpose of NATO was to defend Western Europe against Soviet aggression.

After that time, tension and conflict existed between NATO on one side and the Soviet Union on the other side. There have been no wars between the two parties, but there has been an arms race, and competition to be the leader of the world.

In 1990 the United States and the Soviet Union declared that the Cold War between them was over. But, that does not end conflicts in the world. Wars and rumor of wars have their root in the "fall of man" recorded in Genesis 3. Wars and sufferings will not end until the second coming of the Lord Jesus Christ.

On the earth humankind is fighting against each other. In the spiritual realm, Archangel Michael and his angels fought Satan and the fallen angels (Daniel 10:13, 20; Revelation 12:7–9). It is also important for Christians to realize that the devil is eager to wage war against God's children (Ephesians 6:11–12). That is because they do not worship him. When Satan tempted Christ, he offered Jesus the whole world if the Lord would worship him.

In the political arena, one may be conservative, or liberal, or even neutral. But, in the spiritual realm, we have to take a side, either for God or against God, as He commanded, *"You shall have no other gods before me"* (Exodus 20:3).

In some countries, a young man, at a certain age, is required to serve two or three years in the military. In the spiritual world, everyone must engage in spiritual warfare, whether he wants it or not. That means the invisible confrontation between the kingdom of God and the kingdom of darkness.

Paul exhorted Timothy, *"Endure hardship with us like a good soldier of Christ Jesus"* (2 Timothy 2:3). Christians are soldiers of Christ Jesus. As soldiers we must be trained thoroughly, we must be fully equipped to win the battles. The best protection for Christian soldiers is the full armor of God. We cannot put on metal armor to take our stand against the devil's schemes.

1) The Belt of Truth
Whatever God proclaims is true, and He does not lie. As children of the truthful God, we must honor honesty, as our Heavenly Father commands, *"thou shalt not lie."* The apostle James commands us not to be "double-minded," and to purify our hearts first before we draw near to God and resist the devil.

2) *The breastplate of righteousness*
The devil loves to condemn us, and to pull us away from God. He loves to flash back the sins we committed in the past, to prove that we do not deserve to be saved. But, we can tell the devil to get off our back since, *"there is now no condemnation for those who are in Christ Jesus"* (Romans 8:1). However, *"the spirit is willing, but the body is weak,"* and we may sin many times and in many ways. The good news is the Lord Jesus is able to sympathize with our weaknesses. That is not an excuse to keep on sinning. But, we must confess our sins to the Lord and to each other. *"He is faithful and just and will forgive us our sins and purify us from all unrighteousness"* (1 John 1:9–10). Sins that are not confessed will open the door for the devil to steal the abundant life from us.

3) *The feet shod with the preparation of the gospel of peace*
The gospel of peace or the good news regarding the death, the burial and the resurrection of the Lord Jesus, and all of its benefits, restores peace in the whole universe (Ephesians 1:10; 3:10). It reconciles God and man, the Jews and the Gentiles (Ephesians 2:14–18). He who wears the gospel as his shoes, and walks into the enemies' territory is in the process of restoring peace in the world that Satan has ruined.

In the New Testament the Lord Jesus teaches, *"I tell you the truth, if you have faith as small as a mustard seed, you can say to this mountain, 'Move from here to there' and it will move. Nothing will be impossible for you"* (Matthew 17:20).

The shield of faith deals with steadfast trust in the Lord even in adversity. With faith we stand firm against the flaming arrows.

Daniel gives us an account of the three young Jews, Shadrach, Meshach and Abednego who refused to worship the image of gold that king Nabuchadnezzar had set up, at the risk of being thrown into the burning furnace. They said to the king:

> *"If we are thrown into the blazing furnace, the God we serve is able to save us from it, and he will rescue us from your hand, O king. But even if he does not, we want you to know, O king, that we will not serve your gods or worship the image of gold you have set up."*
>
> (Daniel 3:17–18)

Wow! What a great faith! And their faith did save them from the blazing furnace.

4) *The Helmet of Salvation*

Workers wear helmets in areas where the risk is high. Motorcyclists are required to wear helmets to protect their heads in case of accidents. That kind of helmet is necessary for the protection of human life. Some may not like to wear it, but none can deny its usefulness. By the same token, if a plastic or metal helmet can save the body, the helmet of salvation saves the soul. Without it a person will be eternally dead. With the helmet of salvation a person has the right to draw near to God, and to be under His care. When He is with us, who can be against us? No unclean spirits can defeat us. We must wear the helmet of salvation in our spiritual warfare.

In the last two days I've been spiritually attacked. I have to admit that I've given the enemy a chance to put me on the defensive. It is not a happy situation. I'm still fighting off the enemy. For a non-believer, he may enjoy a thought, but for a believer, the thought is evil, and nurturing it is a sin.

The weapon I used was the sword of the Spirit. The Bible teaches me to resist the devil, and he will flee. The Bible also teaches me to put on the breastplate of righteousness. I'm learning how to use the shield of faith to protect myself from the firing arrows. I'm practicing faith, believing that, God is my refuge and strength, an ever-present help in trouble. So I called on Him for help. He is helping, but I have to focus on Him and to rely on His power to overcome the darts of the enemy. *"Above all else guard your heart, for it is the wellspring of life"* (Proverbs 4:23).

5) The Shield of Faith
Jehoshaphat was one of the good kings of Judah. The Bible spoke of him, *"he walked in the ways his father David had followed. He did not consult the Baals but sought the God of his father and followed his commands rather than the practices of Israel"* (2 Chronicles 17:3–4).

One time *"the Moabites and Ammonites with some of the Meunites came to make war on Jehoshaphat"* (2 Chronicles 20:1). Jehoshaphat was outnumbered; the chance of winning was very slim. *"The king resolved to inquire of the LORD, and he proclaimed a fast for all Judah"* (2 Chronicles 20:3). The people of Judah joined the king in seeking the Lord. After praying, Jehoshaphat worshipped God. Then some Levites stood up and praised the LORD with very loud voice (vs. 19).

Early in the morning the king addressed the people:

> *"'Have faith in the LORD your God and you will be upheld; have faith in his prophets and you will be successful.' After consulting the people, Jehoshaphat appointed men to sing to the LORD and to praise him for the splendor of his holiness as they went out at the head of the army, saying: 'Give thanks to the LORD, for his love endures forever.'"*
> (2 Chronicles 20:20–21)

Their faith touched the Lord's heart, and He defeated their enemies.

6) The Sword of the Spirit—The Word of God
A soldier cannot engage in battle without his weapon; it is simple, but very true. It is a defensive and offensive weapon.

Three synoptic gospels narrated the temptation of the Lord Jesus. His powerful weapon was the word of God. "What would Jesus do?" That is the question we refer to when we don't know what to do. If the Lord Jesus won the battle having the Word of God as His sole weapon, we too can win the spiritual warfare, using the same powerful tool.

Other Powers

Angels: God's Power Manifested

*W*e may not have encountered angels, but the Bible teaches about angels. They are greater than man in power and might (2 Peter 2:11). Their activities reveal the Lord's powers.

In Genesis 18 the Scripture says, *"Then the LORD rained down burning sulfur on Sodom and Gomorrah—from the LORD out of the heavens"* (Genesis 19:24–25). According to the Scripture God himself executes the judgment. But, if He did that by Himself, why were the angels present? The fact that three angels appeared to Abraham and to Lot indicates that the Lord was the Supreme Judge and the angels were the agents of the judgment. The angel's power was also seen in 2 Kings 19, *"That night the angel of the LORD went out and put to death a hundred and eighty-five thousand men in the Assyrian camp. When the people got up the next morning-there were all the dead bodies"* (2 Kings 19:35–36).

The angels do not own any power; they only receive it when the Lord releases His to them. They can do great and mighty things when they do his bidding, when they obey His word, and when they do His will (Psalm 103:20).

Angels are supernatural because they are mightier than men. They can open the prison doors (Acts 5:19; 12:5–11), deliver God's messages (Acts 10:3–4; 23:9; 27:23), and execute judgments (Acts 12:23). They struck the Sodomites who harassed them with blindness (Genesis 19:10–11).

In Revelation the apostle John saw four angels standing at the four corners of the earth, holding back the four winds of the earth (7:1).

The Lord Jesus has a special angel that He calls "my angel" (Revelation 22:16).

Power of the Son

If we believe Jesus Christ is the Son of God we must believe that He has great and mighty power in His hands. He has enough power to overcome the world, *"In (this) world you will have tribulation, but be in good cheer, I have overcome the world"* (John 16:33—NKJV). Is it encouraging? Is it good enough for us to take Him as Lord and Savior?

We are living in a fallen world where difficulties and struggles cannot be avoided. We can face them, we can deal with them, and we can be victorious in God the Son.

Christian messages to the world are not only that we can be saved to go to heaven, but also that we can be delivered from the sufferings of this world. One of the goals of Christian churches is to prepare people for eternity. Christians enjoy life on earth, for the kingdom of God is in His children.

Christians, our Lord has overcome the world, so, with His

power we can overcome trials and tribulations. It's not easy, but it is possible for those who put their trust in Him. *"Be in good cheer!"* Yes, if He says so, do not argue.

When the Lord Jesus gave out His invitation, *"Come to me, all you who are weary and burdened, and I will give you rest"* (Matthew 11:28), He knows what he is talking about. He implies He has the power to take care of all our problems. Paul confirms that truth in the Epistle to the Philippians, *"And my God will meet all your needs according to his glorious riches in Christ Jesus"* (Philippians 4:19).

The story recorded in the Book of Matthew is an illustration of that power in the Lord Jesus:

> *"Just then a woman who had been subject to bleeding for twelve years came up behind him and touched the edge of his cloak. She said to herself, "If I only touch his cloak, I will be healed." Jesus turned and saw her. "Take heart, daughter," he said, "your faith has healed you." And the woman was healed from that moment."*
> (Matthew 9:20–22)

Sometimes we do not need to ask Him to do things for us, but rather we need to reach out to Him, and touch Him, then His power will come out from Him. That power will meet all our needs. Is it wonderful? Is it the key to a successful victorious Christian life?

People may object, "I don't care about the power, I know I'm saved, and I will go to heaven. I just love the Lord. That's all." I totally agree with that statement. But, why not enjoy an abundant life on earth? Does He not say, *"I have come that they may have life, and have it to the full"* (John 10:10)?

The Bible tells us that, after the crippled woman was healed from her infirmity, *"immediately she straightened up and praised God"* (Luke 13:13).

God created human beings so he could enjoy them, and also to enjoy their praise, *"But You are holy, enthroned in the praises of Israel"* (Psalm 22:3—NKJV). The Lord loves to bless us with abundant life, so that we can rejoice in Him, and praise Him.

The Gospel of Jesus, the Power of God

In his epistle to the Romans the apostle declares, *"I am not ashamed of the gospel, because it is the power of God for the salvation of everyone who believes: first for the Jew, then for the Gentile"* (Romans 1:16).

When we read through the books of the Old Testament, it seems like God was harsh unto His people. But, when we consider the causes of His wrath we will see that God's people gave Him a tough time. They disobeyed Him, they turned away from Him, and they left Him for other gods. But, He always showed His mercy to His people. God tried and tried to bring His people back to Him through his prophets and sacrificial offerings.

Since they are the chosen people God gave them a set of laws. They were required to obey His laws. As we have seen, they deliberately failed Him and miserably failed to follow His laws.

There seemed to be a period of four hundred years when God resolved to not have anything to do with His stubborn people. For four centuries He did not communicate with His people. We don't know whether His people cared to seek Him, or to hear from Him.

Finally, by 6 b.c. God broke the silence. He spoke through a New Testament prophet, John the Baptizer—I prefer this name to 'the Baptist'—since he baptized people. As predicted by the prophet Isaiah, he was *"A voice of one calling in the desert, 'Prepare the way for the Lord, make straight paths for him'"* (Matthew 3:3). John prepared the way for the One who came after him, but He would be greater than him. John admitted that he was not worthy to untie the sandals of that Person. John baptized with water, but the One who came after him would baptize with the Holy Spirit. That Person is no one other than God Himself because He is called "Wonderful Counselor, Mighty God, Everlasting Father, Prince of Peace."

Our finite mind cannot understand why the Holy Creator has to be born as a human being, live as a human being, and die for the sins of humankind. However, He inspires the Bible writers to explain to us why He did what He did. He also opens our hearts so we understand that truth, and believe.

What God wants to do is to save us from the sin that entered the world through Adam. In the Old Testament the law required the sacrifice of animals for the forgiveness of sin. Many hundred thousand of animals were sacrificed so that God's people could be reconciled to Him. That was only temporary until the ultimate sacrifice of the Lord Jesus. When He offered Himself, He sacrificed for our sins once and for all.

That is the power of the Gospel that will save all who believe in Jesus Christ. Paul declares, *"Salvation is found in no one else, for there is no other name under heaven given to men by which we must be saved"* (Acts 4:12). The name of Jesus is above all names, *"that at the name of Jesus every knee should bow, in heaven and on earth and under the earth, and every tongue confess that Jesus Christ is Lord, to the glory of God the Father"* (Philippians 2:10–11).

This morning I read a Vietnamese Newsletter in which a Pastor writes a story of a man and a woman. Both left Viet Nam and went to work in Korea. They were both married, but their spouses were not with them. They needed each other, so they lived together. Last year they were saved, and knew that their relationship was not right according to God. They made the right decision to terminate their sinful relationship. They shared the good news to their spouses who became saved by the grace of God, and by the power of the gospel of the Lord Jesus.

I just received a book written by an old friend about an eastern religion. It is very well written. He must have spent a lot of time and energy on it. I read the index and a few pages. The writing is full of religious terms, and hard to understand. It is very impressive. However, it is nothing compared to the gospel of the Lord Jesus. It is sad to hear the word of the apostle Paul, *"The god of this age has blinded the minds of unbelievers, so that they cannot see the light of the gospel of the glory of Christ, who is the image of God"* (2 Corinthians 4:4).

And today, the 27th of June in the year of the Lord 2005, I went to the funeral of a member of a senior citizen club. A group of religious officials officiated at the ceremony, and the monks were chanting the same verse over and over. I didn't know if anyone understood what the chanting was about. I didn't know if anyone knew the purpose of the chanting. I think the chanting may comfort the members of the deceased's family. One good thing I did at that funeral was to pray for that family.

I am thankful because I believe Jesus, who is the image of God. I am glad that I can see the light of the gospel of the glory of Christ.

And today, the 7th of July, my wife and I just got back from a nursing home that we visit once a week. A lady, who has been bedridden for the last three years, is passing away. She suffered a stroke so severe that she could not speak, she could not eat, and she could not turn herself.

She could recover slowly, or at least sit up in a wheelchair. With physical therapy she could learn to talk. However, someone who came to visit her stated that she could never be healed. Unfortunately, she believed the lie, and refused any physical therapy.

At first, my wife offered to read the Bible; she shook her head. My wife kept on visiting her, and the Lord worked with her, and finally, she wished to listen to the Bible reading. My wife read the Bible to her, explained the salvation by trusting the Lord Jesus. When my wife asked if she believes in the Lord Jesus she nodded her head. From that time on, whenever my wife came to see her, she pointed at the Bible, requesting my wife to read the Scripture to her. When my wife wanted to stop she made sign to my wife to continue reading.

This evening, when we came in, her son told us that she is passing away. We heard the chanting from a religious cassette tape. We explained to her son that she believes in Jesus Christ, and will be with Him in heaven.

The power of the Gospel does not save us from physical death for natural death has no power over a man's soul. To a non-believer death means punishment; to a believer death is a gain because it means to be with the Lord forever.

The next Sunday, we went to the County Jail to lead a Bible study with the inmates. The lesson was on the new birth. Some questions were asked: What does the phrase "to be born again" mean? Is it important? Are you born again? After the doctrine of new birth was explained, three inmates who were not sure whether they are born again, wished to receive Jesus Christ as Lord and Savior. Hallelujah! That was not planned. That was the power of the Gospel that saves those who believe. We did not study a long time before the Holy Spirit touched the hearts of those inmates. By praying a short sinner's prayer they have passed from death to life.

Yesterday, God convicted an inmate, and he wept. I asked him if I could pray with him. He mumbled something I couldn't hear, but I prayed for him, believing that the Lord knows and will provide all his needs. When we left the jail, an officer commented, "You made him weep." I believe that the Holy Spirit convicted the man, not I.

The Church: The Power of the Son

When the Lord Jesus came to the region of Caesarea Philippi, He gave His disciples a big test. He asked them who people thought He was. Of course nobody had a clue of who He was because none had the Spirit of God in him. One thought He was John the Baptist, others said Elijah, and still others, Jeremiah or one of the prophets.

The first question led way to His second question, *"Who do you say I am,"* (Matthew 16:15)? He asked His own. At that time, I believe, the Lord Jesus wanted to reveal His identity to his inner circle. Only Peter passed the test with the help from God the Father. He answered correctly the tough question, *"You are the Christ, the Son of the Living God."* Based on Peter's answer, the Lord made this powerful statement, *"And I also say to you that you are Peter, and on this rock I will build My church, and the gates of Hades shall not prevail against it"* (16:18).

The Lord Jesus is indeed who He claims He is, because what He said has come to pass. Fifty-three days after the Lord Jesus' resurrection Peter started the first Christian church with an initial membership of three thousand.

And the Church has been growing and growing, in spite of persecutions and oppositions. Many apostles and Church fathers were martyred for the sake of Christ. Nero killed many Christians including Peter and Paul.

However, at the end of the first century Christians were a headache of the Roman government. In fifteen years (from 81a.

d. to 96 a.d.) the Roman emperor Domitian gave out an order to arrest Christians and so the churches faithfully participated in the sufferings of Christ (I Peter 4:12–17; Revelation 2:10). Even one of the cousins of the Emperor was executed, and his wife exiled, maybe because he was converted to Christianity.

In the beginning of the fourth century, in spite of persecutions, Christianity became an active force in the Roman Empire. At first, it had attracted only the poor and the unlearned. Then the moral conduct of Christians became evident. Educated people began to explain the Gospel to the officials in the court and to the members of the imperial family.

The Christian Church slowly but surely has become a grand World Organization with a historical status that no others can match. That is because the Church is built on the solid Rock (petra in Greek). That Rock is the symbol of The Lord in the Old Testament. The word "rock" the Lord Jesus uses implies He is the Rock of salvation as appeared many times in the Old Testament.

At the end of the third century there were approximately five to six million believers, and fifty million by the end of the tenth century. At the beginning of the 19th century approximately two hundred million believed in Jesus Christ.

If the Church of Jesus Christ cannot pass many tough tests, the Lord Jesus is not "the Christ, the Son of the Living God." Time has proved He is truly the Son of God, and God in the flesh.

10

Men of God

The Story of the Patriarch Abraham, Father of great multitude

*I*n this section we will survey the lives of some of the heroes of faith, and we will learn from their experiences how to tap in God's power, and how to live a victorious Christian life. Men and women of God obtain their strength by walking with the Lord. They know how to be in harmony with Him. We will try to do a survey of the lives of some of the great men in the Bible.

Jews, Arabs and Christians should get along well because all of them claim Abraham as their ancestor. Literally speaking, the Patriarch is the father of Isaac who is the forefather of the Jews, and of Ishmael who is the forefather of the Arabs. Abraham is the Christians' forefather due to their faith in God and in the Lord Jesus Christ.

As Paul teaches, *"Consider Abraham: 'He believed God, and it was credited to him as righteousness.' Understand, then, that those who believe are children of Abraham"* (Galatians 3:6–7).

"From UR of the Chaldeans in ancient southern Babylonia (Genesis 11:31) Abram and his family moved north along the trade routes of the ancient world and settled in the flourishing trade center of HARAN, several hundred miles to the northwest." [12] While living in Haran, at the age of 75 Abram received a call from God, *"Leave your country, your people and your father's household and go to the land I will show you"* (Genesis 12:1).

God picked Abram, out of his father's household to be a great name, a great nation, and a vessel of blessing. Maybe Abraham was the only one in his father's household who still believed in the Lord. That could be the reason why God chose Abraham to be the father of His chosen people, and of the Messiah of all nations. One question was asked, "Does a hero make a circumstance, or does a circumstance make a hero?" In other words, does a mere man become a hero because he was in the right place at the right time? Or can a person plan for something to happen as he anticipated so that he can become a hero?

In the life of Abraham we can find twelve key events that revealed his character:

1) Abram Responded to the Call (Genesis 12:1–7)

Have you ever wondered how did God speak to Abram? Did he show up as an angel? Did he hide Himself in a cloud? Did He hide in a bush? According to the Lord Jesus' own word, "God is Spirit," how can Abram hear Him speak? Amazing, isn't it?

Since we, evangelical Christians, believe that the Bible is the very word of God, we must believe that God did literally speak to Abram.

This is a very significant event. The Lord told Abram to go, and he left his family. Today, in Western societies, an eighteen-year-old man or woman moves out of his/her parent's home; that is a normal thing. If they don't want to move out, that is not normal. But, in Biblical times, the family did not only consist of parents and minor children, but all children and grandchildren as well. People at that time were so attached to their extended families that it was hard for them to leave. Abram leaving his country and his father's house was a big decision. No wonder he is known as a hero of faith, the spiritual forefather of all Christians. Abram must have had faith that was bigger than a mustard seed.

Abram's experience indicates that God is a personal God, and that Abram must have had a personal relationship with the Lord. God does not distance Himself from people. He would lower Himself in order to communicate with man. On the other hand, Abram must have been a spiritual man. Else, either God could not have talked to him, or he could not have heard God. That could be the reason God chose him to carry out His purpose.

2) Abram Pitched His Tent and Built an Altar (Genesis 12:8–10)
Building an altar to the Lord matters much to those who love Him. Wycliffe explained as to why Abraham built an altar, "*By erecting an altar, the patriarch proclaimed his allegiance to Jehovah, and by pitching his tents, he publicly declared to all observers that he was taking permanent possession of the land. In these two symbolic acts, Abram revealed his resolute faith in the power of Jehovah of hosts to carry out all His promises.*"[13] The altar is the symbol of the presence of the Lord. When one lives in the Lord's presence, he can be sure that he is under the divine protection. He can say with confidence, "*If God is for us, who can be against us*" (Romans 8:31)?

The Book of Daniel recorded the story of the three young Israelites—Shadrach, Meshach, and Abednego—who was ordered by the powerful king of Babylon, Nebuchadnezzar, to bow down and worship his statue, or to be thrown into a burning fiery furnace. The three young men said to the king:

> "*O Nebuchadnezzar, we have no need to answer you in this matter. If that is the case, our God whom we serve is able to deliver us from the burning fiery furnace, and He will deliver us from your hand, O king. But if not, let it be known to you, O king, that we do not serve your gods, nor will we worship the gold image which you have set up.*"
> (Daniel 3:16–18—NKJV)

The three young men did not literally erect an altar to the Lord, but they did build an altar by being faithful to the true God, and by trusting He would deliver them from the burning furnace. They put their trust in the Great Deliverer. They must have known Psalm 18, "*The LORD is my rock, my fortress and my deliverer; my God is my rock, in whom I take refuge. He is my shield and the horn of my salvation, my stronghold*" (vs. 2).

When one asks the Lord Jesus to forgive his sin and come into his heart to be his Lord and Savior, that person enters a covenantal relationship with Jesus Christ. That person should erect an altar to the Lord, meaning he should proclaim his allegiance to his Savior. By so doing he is not only guaranteed that God will allow him to "*sit (together) in the heavenly places in Christ Jesus*" (Ephesians 2:6-KJV), but also he may receive a whole lot of blessings on the earth. If a person claims he loves God, but is not faithful to the Lord, he is a liar, and cannot receive any blessings from the Giver of the blessings.

3) Abram in Egypt (Genesis 12:10–20)
Abram who, at the age of seventy-five, responded to the call of God, left his country and his father's household, heading to

an unknown destination. At Shechem, *"The LORD appeared to Abram and said, 'To your offspring I will give this land' "* (Genesis 12:7). The Bible said that Abram built an altar there to the Lord. Abram continued to move south toward the hills east of Bethel where he pitched his tent, and erected another altar. At that time he claimed the Promised Land.

Abram continued to move south toward the Negev.[14] Then came the famine so severe that he had to move out of the land the Lord gave to his offspring.

Abram might ask the Lord, "What's wrong, Lord? Did you say this land belongs to my offspring? Now, how can I and my family survive this famine?" He had to go to Egypt to look for food. He might have inquired of the Lord, or he might not.

4) Fear for his Life (12:10–13:2; 20:12–13)
But, Abram's faith was tested, and he might have had some doubt. Doubt? The one who was known for his faith? Yes, he did not have peace of mind when he asked Sarah to tell people that she was his sister. His doubt almost cost Abram his wife.

We may not be faithful, but the Lord is always faithful as Moses told God's people, *"Know therefore that the LORD your God is God; he is the faithful God, keeping his covenant of love to a thousand generations of those who love him and keep his commands"* (Deuteronomy 7:9–10). For a short while when Abram had made a decision based on his own wisdom, he might not have felt the presence of the Lord in his life. However, the Lord was there, because He is Jehovah Shamma (the Lord is there). Because the Lord is faithful, He stopped Pharaoh from taking Sarah as his wife. Abram left Egypt, richer than when he came.[15]

5) It Was Difficult (13:5–12)
Do we need to inquire of the Lord all the time, for all things? Paul

advises all the saints in Christ Jesus at Philippi, *"Do not be anxious about anything, but in everything, by prayer and petition, with thanksgiving, present your requests to God"* (Philippians 4:6). Paul means we should inquire of the Lord in everything.

We cannot know whether Abram consulted the Lord when he decided to go to Egypt, or to separate from Lot. In those two instances he had no other choices. We may say that God gives us the wisdom, the ability to think, and to make a right decision. Of course we may go to Him for help when we need His direction.

We've seen that Abram did not make the right decision when he did not tell the whole truth about Sarai. However, since he had a covenant relationship with God, the Lord worked for the good of Abram in everything.

That statement is true when Abram decided to yield to Lot the right to pick the land. According to the world, that was not a smart thing to do. But it was wise in God's sight.

6) *Family Matters (14:1–17)*

As recorded in the Book of Genesis, Lot and his family were taken captives by the four kings. Who could rescue Lot if not his uncle Abram? We may not see it, but it was only with God's help that Abram could *"attack them (the four kings) and he routed them, pursuing them as far as Hobah, north of Damascus. He recovered all the goods and brought back his relative Lot and his possessions, together with the women and the other people"* (Genesis 14:15).

That was not the only time Abram delivered his nephew. The second time, without Abram's intercession Lot and his family could not have escaped the burning sulfur rained down on Sodom and Gomorrah.

7) *Setting an Example (14:18–20)*

After Abram had defeated Kedorlaomer and his allies, the king of Sodom and the king of Salem came out to meet him in the King's Valley.

There are some facts that deserve to be noted. First, Melchizedek, king of Salem brought out bread and wine. "The name of this mysterious person means either 'king of righteousness,' or, 'my king is righteousness,' or, 'my king is Zedek.' Zedek is the Hebrew word for 'righteousness,' and also the name of a Canaanite deity." [16] He was the priest-king of Salem, which means the city of peace. He was the type of Christ who is "a priest forever in the order of Melchizedek" (Hebrews 5:6). Second, bread and wine "were tokens of friendship and hospitality. Melchizedek praised El Elyon, his God (AV, the most high God) for granting Abram the power to achieve victory. Abram recognized Melchizedek's (El Elyon) as Jehovah, the God he himself served." [17] The king of Salem supplied refreshment and sustenance for the victor and his weary men. But, there was something deeper than food and drink. That was the type of sacrament as our present church communion where the "priest," or clergy serves the Lord's Table with bread and wine—that can mean "new wine," or grape juice. By serving bread and wine Melchizedek thanked the Most High God for Abram's victory. Actually, that was God's feast, and He received all the credit.

Today, most Christian Churches serve Communion on the first Sunday of the month when the congregation brings in the tithes and offerings as the first fruits of their labor.

8) *Wise Decision (14:21–24)*

In Genesis 14 we met another interesting personality, the king of Sodom. As a defeated king he had no right to ask Abram for anything. But he said to Abram, "*Give me the people and keep the goods for you*" (Genesis 14:21). But the patriarch refused to take anything from the king except for the food his men had eaten, because Abram did not want the king to be able to say, "I made Abram rich."

We have seen that Abram made mistakes. But on the above two occasions the patriarch was praiseworthy, for he knew his responsibilities toward God, and had the right attitude toward man. As the winner Abram had the right to take everything, but he showed grace to the king of Sodom by giving everything to the king. Today, when a Christian is close to the Lord he may be more and more like his Savior.

9) *A Man of Faith May Not Understand Everything (15:5; 17:1–21)*

We cannot measure faith, or weigh faith, and that's why the Lord Jesus does not require a lot of it from us. He says that we only need faith as big as a mustard seed, and it will do a lot for us. We don't need to understand, but we need to have faith.

After Abram had gone through quite a great experience, the Lord asserted that He is Abram's shield and exceedingly great reward. Abram did not understand what that would do for him, and expressed his concern for an heir.

10) *Obedience (17:9–27)*

Fifteen years had passed from chapter twelve to chapter seventeen. Abram had gone through the trial period. The Lord confirmed His covenant with the patriarch. Circumcision was the sign of the covenant. Abram prostrated before God as a sign of his submission and acceptance of the covenant. His name was changed from "exalted father" to Abraham, or "father of many nations." The name Sarai was also changed to Sarah, which means "princess." They became two new persons.

One detail in this story is worth noting. After God had confirmed His covenant with Abram, and promised a son to Abram, the patriarch still could not believe what he had heard. As a matter of fact, he said to himself, "*Will a son be born to a man a hundred years old? Will Sarah bear a child at the age of ninety*" (Genesis 17:17–18)?

That is the reason why the Lord Jesus only requires us to have faith as big as a mustard seed which was the smallest seed in the Biblical times.

11) Intercession (18:17–33)

Chapter eighteen shows Abraham as an intercessor. He did not intercede for his own people, but for the ungodly. Abraham could know what was going on around him; he could have known how wicked were Sodom and Gomorrah. He would be glad he had not chosen to live there. He still had compassion for those two cities, and he pleaded for them. Of course he was concerned for his nephew. But, instead of praying for Lot and his family alone, Abraham interceded for the entire cities.

Even though God did not grant Abraham's request that was not a reason not to pray. He set an example for all Christians to pray for everybody, including the lost. Christians have privileges that non-believers do not have; they are to enter into the Holy of Holies, and to present our requests unto the Lord. If we fail to pray we forfeit our rights, just as some citizens do not exercise their right to vote.

12) Patience (21:1–6)

Finally Abraham and Sarah had a son as the Lord had promised them ten years previously. By that time they had learned the lesson of patience. They knew that the Lord was faithful. They were happy because their lifetime dream came true. It was possible for them to be a great nation, even though they did not fully understand it.

13) The Test (chapter 22)
In chapter 22 Abraham was given a very rough test. A great man stands out only after being tested. He passed the test gloriously. God commended Abraham for trusting him:

> "*I swear by myself, declares the LORD, that because you have done this and have not withheld your son, your only son, I will surely bless you and make your descendants as numerous as the stars in the sky and as the sand on the seashore. Your descendants will take possession of the cities of their enemies, and through your offspring all nations on earth will be blessed, because you have obeyed me.*"
> (Genesis 22:16–18)

From the life of the patriarch we can draw some practical lessons for us. Abraham was a great man of faith and was considered as the forefather of the Jews and of the Muslims, and the spiritual forefather of all Christians. More people today know of him than any other great leaders of the world. He was not perfect, and had some doubts, and fear. The great test he passed was to offer his son for sacrifice at the command of the Lord. Perfect submission and perfect obedience are required of all Christians.

Jacob, that supplants

1) The Escape
Jacob was a type of "homebody," minding the flocks and household duties. By buying his brother's birthright and stealing the blessings which his father intended for Esau, Jacob showed that he was not only interested in the earthly things. But, Jacob used the wrong means to reach his goal. That was out of God's will. He

should have waited for God's time and God's way to receive the blessing God had promised.

Jacob was predestined to inherit the Lord's blessing, "the older (Esau) will serve the younger (Jacob)." But, because he did not go along with God's will, he had to flee with only the staff in his hand.

2) The Vision

When Jacob started to realize that his flight was the consequence of his deceit, the Lord drew the patriarch close by a vision of the ladder set up on earth, with the top reaching to heaven.

Graciously, the Lord promised Jacob (1) the land and (2) universal blessing to all families of the earth.[18] Meanwhile, he would have (1) God's presence, (2) God's protection, (3) restoration to home, (4) unfailing faithfulness.

God's manifestation touched Jacob. He seemed to know the Lord better. Then, he made his stony pillow into a pillar, consecrated with oil. He also vowed to give back a tenth of everything the Lord would give him.

3) Sowing and Reaping

Jacob came to Padan Aram where he found his uncle Laban, a man who was more clever than him. There, Jacob worked for his uncle for seven years for Leah, Laban's older daughter, whom he did not love. He had deceived his father and brother, now his uncle deceived him. He reaped what he sowed.

4) God's Plan

Even though God's people are not exempt from chastisement, God is faithful in fulfilling His promises.

Jacob was in Padan Aram for forty years. He worked fourteen years in order to marry Laban's two daughters, and six years to raise Laban's cattle. For the last twenty years Jacob worked to build an asset for himself.

At the end of forty years of labor, Jacob left Laban with two wives, twelve sons, two maidservants, many hundreds of servants, and many flocks, and herds, and camels.

5) *The Wrestling for a Blessing*

Jacob was about to be home after forty years in exile. He thought it would be a happy moment if his brother Esau did not come to meet him. Forty years had passed, but the threat of his brother still haunted Jacob. He hadn't changed much. He made plans to protect himself against his brother's revenge. Here we see Jacob praying—he may not have prayed for a long time—"*Save me, I pray, from the hand of my brother Esau, for I am afraid he will come and attack me and also the mothers with their children*" (Genesis 32:11).

His prayer was answered, and Jacob met with the Angel of Jehovah. Again he showed a hunger for blessing, and did not quit wrestling until he got what he wished. He was blessed indeed because Esau apparently forgave and forgot, "*But Esau ran to meet Jacob and embraced him; he threw his arms around his neck and kissed him. And they wept*" (Genesis 33:4).

6) *Real change*

After Jacob met with God, and reconciled with his brother Esau, he pitched his tent at Shechem in Canaan. "*There he set up an altar and called it El Elohe Israel*" (33:20).

Then, Jacob heard from God, "*Go up to Bethel and settle there, and build an altar there to God, who appeared to you when you were fleeing from your brother Esau*" (35:1). At that time Jacob decided to surrender totally to God, he ordered his family to get rid of all foreign gods.

I believe that from that moment Jacob had no other gods before Jehovah, God started to bring Jacob into His plan of salvation: the Messiah comes from the line of Judah, one of Jacob's sons.

Joseph, remover or increaser, The Power of Dream

Many talented young men and young ladies in America are labeled "American Idols." They are idols all right, but not models. When we take a look at the life of Joseph we see many characteristics that make him a man we should not only look up, but also follow in his footsteps.

1) A Man with a Vision

Psychologically speaking, many positive factors contributed to the success of Joseph. First, the "richly ornamented robe" boosted his self-image. It made him feel very special among his brothers. Second, his two dreams confirmed his future leadership position. His account did not reveal that Joseph had a burning desire to be over his brothers. His robe and his dreams must have sunk deep into Joseph's consciousness and given him spiritual and psychological strength to endure many trials and tribulations.

2) Man of Integrity

Joseph had had a dream, and he could not be happy just being a slave like hundreds of others in Potiphar's mansion. Joseph knew that in order to climb up the ladder he must study Egyptian. Evidently, after a short time in Egypt, he mastered the language that would be required for the position of attendant.

As the beloved son of Jacob, Joseph must have learned from his father godly principles, which he held to overcome temptation. In addition to integrity, Joseph was a man of loyalty. Since Potiphar trusted him with everything, he could not betray his master. When Potiphar's wife seduced him, Joseph refused, *"No one is greater in this house than I am. My master has withheld nothing from me except you, because you are his wife. How then could I do such a wicked thing and sin against God?"* (Genesis 39:9). Joseph knew that, to be the man God wanted him to be, he could not compromise his moral values, or reduce God's standards to a human level.

3) A Man of Peace
Falsely accused and unjustly thrown in jail, Joseph kept his faith in the God of his fathers.

"Now faith is being sure of what we hope for and certain of what we do not see." (Hebrews 11:1)

Joseph, instead of having a "pity party," kept his perfect peace, knowing what would be the outcome. He got along well with God's providence, patiently waiting for his dream to come true.

4) The Interpreter of Dream
The Bible tells us that the Lord was with Joseph and gave him success in everything he did. Even when Joseph was in prison *"the LORD was with him; he showed him kindness and granted him favor in the eyes of the prison warden"* (Genesis 39:22).

Joseph's dreams started to come true when Potiphar put him in charge of the household. It appeared that Joseph was never a slave. Evidently, God's plan for Joseph slowly unfolded. If Potiphar's wife had been faithful to her husband Joseph would be his master's attendant for life, thus he could not have saved his family. Joseph might have asked the Lord, "Why Lord? Why am I in prison for something I didn't do? That is not fair!" Our Lord, in the Garden of Gethsemane might ask of God the Father, "Abba Father, why me? Why do I have to die for the sins of the world?"

Even a prophet like Habakkuk could not understand why God kept silent before social injustice.

In prison Joseph had a chance to interpret dreams, and later he was introduced to Pharaoh as a dream interpreter. Joseph advised Pharaoh, *"And now let Pharaoh look for a discerning and wise man and put him in charge of the land of Egypt"* (41:33). Pharaoh looked around his court and found no man more discerning and wiser than Joseph.

> *"Then Pharaoh said to Joseph, 'Since God has made all this known to you, there is no one so discerning and wise as you. You shall be in charge of my palace, and all my people are to submit to your orders. Only with respect to the throne will I be greater than you."*
>
> (41:39–40)

Joseph's first dream was literally fulfilled in Genesis 42 when Joseph's brothers arrived, they bowed down to him with their faces to the ground (vs. 6b).

Moses, taken out, drawn forth

God spoke to Jeremiah, *"Before I formed you in the womb I knew you, before you were born I set you apart; I appointed you as a prophet to the nations"* (Jeremiah 1:5). That may also be true with Moses. As a matter of fact, when Moses was still in his mother's womb, Pharaoh had already given him the death sentence by giving an order to the Hebrew midwives Shiphrah and Puah: *"When you help the Hebrew women in childbirth and observe them on the deliv-*

In Harmony With God

ery stool, if it is a boy, kill him; but if it is a girl, let her live" (Exodus 1:16).

But, Moses did not die because the "I AM WHO I AM" had set him apart, and appointed him a prophet. The Lord had a grand job for Moses, so He arranged for the princess of Egypt to go down to the Nile to bathe. On the river she found a baby floating in a papyrus basket. God saved Moses for a second time to be his servant.

Like Jacob, Moses had to flee for his life, and to be in exile for forty years. The Bible does not tell us what happened during those forty years. Moses' life may have been very simple. He married Zipporah, the daughter of a priest of Midian. He did not build for himself great wealth like Jacob, however, when he tended the sheep of his father-in-law Jethro, he was really blessed because he could spend time with God. He also had time to study the region of Aqaba through which he would lead the Israelites to the Promised Land.

When Moses might have felt comfortable with his life, even though he might not have forgotten the crime he committed forty years before, the Lord appeared to him in a burning bush.

"Moses, Moses," God called Moses. "Who is calling me?" Moses asked. "Me, but first you need to take off your sandals," the Lord replied, "for your are standing on holy ground." The Lord continued, "Moses, you have been here for forty years already. You look bored, are you? I have an important job for you." "Yes, Lord, speak, I'm listening." And God spoke "I want you to go back to Egypt and take my people out of there because they are in bondage."

It amazes me that there are not two drops of water similar; there are not two identical people. When the Lord commanded Abram to leave his country, his people and his parents, Abram did as the Lord had told him. As for Moses, he gave every excuse possible to turn down the job God offered him. To me, his excuse was that he was afraid to return to the land where forty years ago he had committed a crime. I don't think Moses lacked confidence since he grew up and was educated as a prince.

From the book of Exodus we have learned that Moses was a great leader. God knew the ability of His man when He called Moses. God worked miracles through His servant. Moses was successful because he was in the Lord's presence. God spoke directly to him. He was a liaison between God and the people. Moses lived in harmony with God. However, all have sinned, the Bible says. Only one time Moses didn't obey the Lord, and he was penalized: he was not allowed to enter the Promised Land.

Joshua, savior, deliverer

Joshua son of Nun was famous because of his great faith. He was one of the twelve Jewish spies sent into the land to get information for Moses, so the Commander-in-Chief could decide on the strategy for his operation. The Bible says, *"The righteous shall walk by faith."* Twelve spies returned and reported to Moses and to the Israelites. Ten of them didn't think they should conquer the land that was occupied by giants, and they were just like grasshoppers. Joshua and Caleb didn't agree with the other ten comrades, *"Only do not rebel against the LORD. And do not be afraid of the people of the land, because we will swallow them up. Their protection is gone, but the LORD is with us. Do not be afraid of them"* (Number 14:9).

Because God's people didn't trust and obey Him, those who were twenty years old and older were not allowed to enter the land filled with milk and honey. Since they were not in accord with God they could not inherit their portion. The spiritual application of this story is that those who do not put their trust in God's only begotten Son will not enter heaven, the spiritual Promised Land. Joshua believed in God; not only could he enter the Promised Land, but also possessed it.

Elijah, God the Lord

James recorded Elijah's effective prayer that moved God to withhold rain for three years and a half. How was his prayer effectual? James also explained that the prophet was righteous, and that he didn't ask with wrong motives.

Fausset speaks of the prophet: "His burning zeal, bluntness of address, fearlessness of man, were nurtured in lonely communion with God, away from the polluting court, amidst his native wilds." [19]

In First Kings Elijah had bad news to tell King Ahab. Then the Lord told him to turn eastward, and hide in the Kerith Ravine, east of the Jordan. There the Lord ordered the ravens to feed him. *"So he did what the LORD had told him. He went to the Kerith Ravine, east of the Jordan, and stayed there. The ravens brought him bread and meat in the morning and bread and meat in the evening, and he drank from the brook"* (1 Kings 17:5–6).

Bread and meat may not be great meals for us today, but must have been a blessing to Elijah during the famine. After a year the brook dried up. He retreated to Sarepta or Sarephath where a poor widow gave him a cake made with the last handful of flour and the little oil she had left.

God repaid the widow for her faith and generosity more than she could imagine. First, the Bible says, *"The jar of flour will not be used up and the jug of oil will not run dry until the day the LORD gives rain on the land"* (1 Kings 17:14). Second, her son was resurrected.

The above records are nothing compared to Elijah's confrontation with four hundred and fifty prophets of Baal.

After being in hiding for three years Elijah went to present himself to King Ahab at the command of the Lord. After he had presented himself to the king he asked the king to summon the people from all over Israel to meet him on Mount Carmel. He also requested the king to bring the four hundred and fifty prophets of Baal and the four hundred prophets of Asherah, who ate at Jezebel's table.

The rest of chapter 18 of First Kings describes how Elijah challenged the prophets of Baal and slaughtered them in Kishon Valley. The last verse of chapter 18 says, *"The power of the LORD came upon Elijah and, tucking his cloak into his belt, he ran ahead of Ahab all the way to Jezreel"* (1 Kings 18:46).

Since the prophets of Baal were Queen Jezebel's protégés, the Queen vowed to take revenge. Elijah had to flee for his life. As a Vietnamese proverb advises, "Out of thirty-six alternatives, running will be the best." The Bible says there is a season to everything: there is a time to win; there is a time to run. In this case he had to run in order for the Lord to protect him.

Elijah was so depressed he prayed that he might die. But, God had not finished with him yet, and the Lord sent an angel to serve him food. After showing His glory the Lord sent Elijah back to the wilderness of Damascus to anoint Hazael king over Syria, Jehu ... over Israel, and Elisha ... prophet. Of those three duties, the most important was to anoint Elisha, the son of Shaphat as prophet in his stead.

Second Kings 1 described how Elijah called the fire to come down from heaven to consume a company of fifty men with its captain. How could he do that? Because he was God's agent, he was allowed to ask for divine support, just as a commander of an army can ask for support from the Air Force or the Navy to win a battle. After Elijah had accomplished his mission, a chariot of fire and horses of fire appeared, and the man of God went up to heaven in a whirlwind. That is the illustration of the rapture that Paul teaches in I Thessalonians 4, *"After that, we who are still alive and are left will be caught up together with them in the clouds to meet the Lord in the air. And so we will be with the Lord forever"* (1 Thessalonians 4:17).

A man of God is not necessarily always dancing on the mountaintop. Sometimes he slips down to the low valley, but God meets him there, taking him by the hand, and they go up again.

Elisha, salvation of God

Elisha was plowing with twelve yoke of oxen when Elijah went up to him and threw his cloak around him. This was an investiture with prophetic office. Immediately Elisha responded to the call. He set out to follow Elijah and became his attendant. By slaughtering his yoke of oxen and burning his plowing equipment, he showed he had made up his mind not to return to his old way of living. Elisha had only one plan, and he had no alternative. He must move ahead, no turning back.

The Lord Jesus asks His disciples to deny themselves, to pick up the cross, and follow Him. The apostle Paul decided to forget what was behind, and press on toward the goal to win the prize for which God had called him heavenward in Christ Jesus.

I myself failed in doing something because I didn't do it with determination. Successful people invest everything they have in what they want to do.

"But whatever was to my profit I now consider loss for the sake of Christ" (Philippians 3:7).

Elisha grew up in a God-fearing family that was very favorable for the producing of God's prophet.

The Book of Second Kings describes how Elijah was taken up to heaven in a whirlwind, and Elisha was tenacious in the pursuit of his office. Three times Elijah told the young disciple to stay behind, but Elisha was determined to cleave to his master. The reason was that he wanted to "inherit a double portion of Elijah's spirit," meaning he really wanted the office of prophet.

Elisha's persistence did pay off. Elijah went up to heaven; Elisha picked up the cloak that had fallen from his master. With that cloak the young prophet performed his first miracle by dividing the Jordan, and he crossed over the river. That was how he began his ministry, and other prophets acknowledged his office, *"The company of the prophets from Jericho, who were watching, said, 'The spirit of Elijah is resting on Elisha.' And they went to meet him and bowed to the ground before him"* (2 Kings 2:15).

Elisha performed more and greater miracles than his predecessor, including:
- The healing of Naaman the commander of the army of the king of Aram (2 Kings 5);
- The deliverance of the king of Israel, of the king of Judah and of the king of Edom from the hand of Moab by giving them water.

David, well-beloved

The statement of the Lord Jesus, "I am the Root and the offspring of David," and the title "Son of David" tells how important this man is.

When David was tending his father's sheep, his father asked him to go to the front line and visit his brothers who were fighting against the Philistines. When he arrived at the camp he ran to his brothers. As they were talking *"Goliath the Philistine champion from Gath, stepped out from his lines and shouted his usual defiance, and David heard it*" (1 Samuel 17:23). The Israelites ran from the giant in great fear. David did not have any combat experience, but he seemed not intimidated by this giant. He wanted to know what would be the reward for the man who killed the Philistine champion. David was thinking about overcoming the uncircumcised Philistine who dared to defy the army of God. It may be OK if Goliath defied David. This verse of Psalm 69, "*for zeal for your house consumes me, and the insults of those who insult you fall on me*" (vs. 9) applies to David when he wanted to stand up for the Lord's army. His faith in God gave him strength to knock down the giant. That is faith, believing that he fights not for him, but for the Lord, and God will give him the victory, no matter how big the giant is, "*If God is for us, who can be against us.*"

The second characteristic of David to be noted as he was consistent with his principle, "to never touch the Lord's anointed." No matter how badly Saul treated David, he never took revenge.

One time David and his men were hiding in a cave, and Saul went in to relieve himself. David had a chance to get rid of this enemy who had looked for every opportunity to take David's life. Yet, David only crept up unnoticed and cut off a corner of Saul's robe. Still David considered this act as inappropriate behavior toward the anointed of God, "*He said to his men, 'The LORD forbid that I should do such a thing to my master, the LORD's anointed, or lift my hand against him; for he is the anointed of the LORD*'" (1 Samuel 24:5–6).

After Saul had left, David went out of the cave and called out to him, "*My lord the king . . .*" "*When Saul looked behind him, David bowed down and prostrated himself with his face to the ground*" (24:8). Then David showed Saul the piece of robe in his hand, and told Saul that he would not touch him. David is a good example to those who are under authority. He also set an example for those who are in a leadership position.

When David heard the news that "the Philistines were fighting against Keilah and were looting the threshing floors," he inquired of the LORD, saying, "Shall I go and attack these Philistines" (1 Sam 23:1–2). The answer was affirmative, but his men doubted. Once again, David inquired of the Lord, *"and the LORD answered him, 'Go down to Keilah, for I am going to give the Philistines into your hand'"* (23:4). Not every one is a born leader. A great leader, of course, must possess a gift, but he is not necessarily on top of everything. Some of the time he has important decisions to make, and doesn't know what to do. At that time, it is wise to inquire of the Lord.

David didn't know what to do. He asked the Lord, and the Lord told him. *"So David and his men went to Keilah, fought the Philistines and carried off their livestock. He inflicted heavy losses on the Philistines and saved the people of Keilah"* (1 Sam 23:5). The omniscient God has all the information we need to make good decisions. Leaders, go to Him as often as you can. If you don't make time to inquire of the Lord, you will take your chances.

David was a great man, a man "after God's own heart." People today still love him, and admire him. However, he was human like all of us, for the Bible asserts, "All have sinned and come short of the glory of God." David inquired of the Lord when the situation was critical. When he sent for Bathsheba, when he sent for Uriah, when he ordered Joab to put Uriah in the front line, he did not inquire of the Lord.

Even though David was a man after God's own heart, he was not exempt from the consequences of his sin. His family became "dysfunctional," starting with the death of the child that Uriah's wife had borne to him. Next, one of his sons Amnon, assaulted Tamar, his daughter from another wife. Two years later Tamar's brother Absalom, plotted to kill all the king's other sons. But, only

Amnon was killed. That was not the end. Absalom had his eyes on the throne of his father. He succeeded in putting David on the run. After taking the capital, Absalom, at the advice of Ahithophel, he lay with his father's concubines in the sight of all Israel.

However, when Nathan the prophet exposed David's adultery, the king was quick to acknowledge that he had sinned against the Lord. It does not matter how many times a person has failed God, a true believer heeds the Lord's teaching. The Latin expression "mea culpa," it's my fault, should be the first reaction of a spiritual man.

David suffered the consequences of his sin against the Lord, but God is faithful. Absalom won a battle, but David won the war for he was the anointed of God.

I can identify myself with him, but I cannot compare with him on many aspects, in particular his love for God.

In spite of his imperfection, David was a great man of God, because he was a man after God's own heart. David was the standard with which his successors were evaluated. A king of Judah was considered to be good when "he walked in the former ways of his father David."

Solomon, peaceable, perfect, one who recompenses

The Bible teaches, *"In his heart a man plans his course, but the LORD determines his steps"* (Proverbs 16:9).

When King David was advanced in age, Adonijah "put himself forward and said, 'I will be king.' So he got chariots and horses ready, with fifty men to run ahead of him" (1 Kings 1:5). Adonijah planned his course. However, as the angels declared to king Nebuchadnezzar, "the Most High is sovereign over the kingdoms of men and gives them to anyone he wishes and sets over them the lowliest of men" (Daniel 4:17). God did not appoint Adonijah to be king of Israel, and He gave the prophet Nathan the wisdom to assist Bathsheba, Solomon's mother. As Nathan had advised, Bathsheba went to see the aged king in his room. King David asked her, *"What is it you want?"* Bathsheba reminded the king, *"Solomon your son shall be king after me, and he will sit on my throne"* (1 Kings 1:17).

While she was still speaking with the king, Nathan the prophet arrived. He confirmed to the king that Adonijah had made himself king. Without delay King David ordered Zadok the priest and Nathan the prophet to take Solomon down to Gihon, a sacred spring in Jerusalem, and anoint him king over Israel. Therefore, Nathan overturned Adonijah's plan. Without his wisdom the history of Israel would have taken another course, and the genealogy of our Lord would read differently.

First Kings 3 tells us, *"Solomon showed his love for the LORD by walking according to the statutes of his father David, except that he offered sacrifices and burned incense on the high places"* (3:3). It appeared that the young king loved the Lord and wished to follow his father David's footsteps. However, he did not follow the laws of Moses.

We know that Solomon loved God when he chose wisdom instead of riches. The Lord bestowed on him wisdom, but the kind of wisdom he asked for was *"nothing more than practical shrewdness, or knowledge of the world and of human nature."* [20]

About Solomon, the International Standard Bible Encyclopaedia comments *"But his whole idea was to secure himself in peace, to amass wealth and indulge his love of grandeur with more than oriental splendor."* [21] Also, according to the above Encyclopedia, Solomon turned the natural bend of the Hebrew people to commerce. *"Solomon had in fact reduced a free people to slavery, and concentrated the wealth of the whole country in the capital. As soon as he was out of the way, his country subjects threw off the yoke and laid claim to their* ancient freedom. His son found himself left with the city and a territory as small as an English county."²²

Most of the time, Solomon used common sense instead of godly sense. First Kings 3 tells us that when the kingdom was firmly established in Solomon's hands, he *"made an alliance with Pharaoh, King of Egypt and married his daughter"* (1 Kings 3:1). In addition to her he married other wives for political reasons, for establishing relations with the neighboring people: the Zidonians, the Hittites and other nationalities (11:1), some of which were forbidden to Israelites (Deuteronomy 7:3). ²³ *"Nevertheless, Solomon held fast to them in love. He had seven hundred wives of royal birth and three hundred concubines, and his wives led him astray"* (1 Kings 11:2–3).

To be fair we should give Solomon credit for the building of the temple which was so magnificent that those built in later times cannot compare. However, we do not know how often King Solomon offered sacrifices and burned incense in the temple of the Lord. Worshipping the Lord in the temple is far better than building the temple.

Toward the end of his life Solomon looked back to his past and made this statement, *"Meaningless! Meaningless! Utterly meaningless! Everything is meaningless"* (Ecclesiastes 1:2). As an experienced old man, Solomon admitted that life was full of deception and vanity. The Book of Ecclesiastes seems to convey a pessimistic worldview. However, it also shows good things man can enjoy. It instructs man to fear God, and to remember that God bestows good things on us.

After presenting all the dark side of life, and what we can do to enjoy a blessed life, the old wise man concluded, *"Now all has been heard; here is the conclusion of the matter: Fear God and keep his commandments, for this is the whole duty of man"* (12:13).

David, the man after God's own heart, died and left behind a

"United Kingdom" to Solomon, as he wrote, "*Surely goodness and mercy shall follow me all the days of my life*" (Psalm 23:6a—NKJV). On the other hand, Solomon's kingdom, after his reign, was not enlarged, but became divided. Was Solomon to be blamed for his not walking with the Lord as his father David had? Maybe not. But the kingdom went downhill until Nabuchadnezzar, the Assyrian despot, put an end to the perfidious and inconstant monarchy of Judah.

It will be interesting to study some of the kings of the Southern kingdom.

Asa, physician (911–870 b.c.)

Asa succeeded Abijah as king. He "cleaned house" by removing idolatry, and "*No one was at war with him during those years, for the LORD gave him rest*" (2 Chronicles 14:6). Asa taught his people a simple truth, "we sought the LORD our God, and he has given us rest on every side."

When Asa faced the vast army and three hundred chariots of Zerah the Cushite, and when he knew that he could not defeat a powerful enemy, he called to the Lord. Because "*Asa did what was good and right in the eyes of the LORD his God the LORD struck down the Cushites before Asa and Judah. The Cushites fled*" ((2 Chronicles 14:2, 12).

I believe that Asa did what was good, but not good enough. To help him do better the Lord sent Azariah son of Oded to remind Asa, "*If you seek him, he will be found by you, but if you forsake him, he will forsake you*" (15:2b), "*But as for you, be strong and do not give up, for your work will be rewarded*" (vs. 7). Encouraged, Asa "*removed the detestable idols from the whole land of Judah and Benjamin and from the towns he had captured in the hills of Ephraim. He repaired the altar of the LORD that was in front of the portico of the LORD's temple"* (vs. 8). Asa was blessed because he was obedient to the word of God. Through him the Lord blessed the entire nation, *"So the LORD gave them rest on every side"* (2 Chronicles 15:15).

In the New Testament the Lord Jesus teaches, *"Anyone who loves his father or mother more than me is not worthy of me; anyone who loves his son or daughter more than me is not worthy of me"* (Matthew 10:37). Asa showed himself worthy of the Lord whom he loved when he *"deposed his grandmother Maacah from her position as queen mother, because she had made a repulsive Asherah pole"* (2 Chronicles 15:16).

I believe that Asa was one of the eight good kings of Judah because he had done right in thirty-six years of his reign. However, he started to go down hill when Baasha king of Israel went up against Judah. Faint-hearted, Asa made an alliance with Benhadad of Damascus, instead of putting his entire trust in the God of his forefathers.

The Lord spoke to Asa through Hanani the seer, *"For the eyes of the LORD range throughout the earth to strengthen those whose hearts are fully committed to him. You have done a foolish thing, and from now on you will be at war"* (16:9). But the king became angry with the seer, instead of humbling himself before the Lord.

In the last two years of his reign king Asa was afflicted with a disease in his feet, and *"Though his disease was severe, even in his illness he did not seek help from the LORD, but only from the physicians"* (16:12).

In the epistle to the Galatians Paul listed nine fruits of the Spirit. To those we may add persistence. Had Asa persisted until the end, he would have been a great king.

Jehoshaphat, Jehovah-judged (870–848 b.c.)

The Scripture says the Lord was with Jehoshaphat because *"he walked in the ways his father David had followed. He did not consult the Baals, but sought the God of his father and followed his commands rather than the practices of Israel"* (2 Chronicles 17:3–4). The king held the key to success. The Lord blessed him, his kingdom was established under his control, and so he had great wealth and honor.

Jehoshaphat sent his officials to teach in the towns of Judah. Because God was with him, the kingdoms of the lands surrounding Judah did not make war with him.

Some Philistines brought Jehoshaphat gifts, and the Arabs brought him flocks. The king became more and more powerful, and had large supplies in the towns of Judah.

People use the saying "like father, like son" to explain why a person behaves the way he does. That is true in the case of Jehoshaphat and of his father Asa. He made a big mistake when he allied with Ahab king of Israel. As an ally Jehoshaphat had to go to war against Ramoth Gilead with Ahab, even when the Lord told them that was not a good idea. Ahab died in the battle, but Jehoshaphat returned safely to his palace in Jerusalem. According to Jehu the seer, Jehoshaphat survived because there was some good in him, for he had rid the land of the Asherah poles, and had set his heart on seeking God. The psalmist wrote, *"The fool says in his heart,'There is no God"* (Psalm 14:1). But God surely rewards those who seek Him.

There is a difference between a spiritual man and a carnal man. The spiritual man gives heed to the Lord, and carnal man ignores His commands. Jehoshaphat had learned his lesson. After coming out of the battle against Ramoth Gilead alive, the king of Judah *"went out again among the people from Beersheba to the hill country of Ephraim and turned them back to the LORD, the God of their fathers"* (2 Chronicles19:4). The spiritual man knows when he goes astray and gets back on the right track.

It's interesting to expound on Jehoshaphat's instructions to the judges he appointed in the land and in each of the fortified cites of Judah, *"Now let the fear of the LORD be upon you. Judge carefully, for with the LORD our God there is no injustice or partiality or bribery"* (2 Chronicles 19. 7). That verse should be framed and hung on the walls of all the Court Houses of all nations of the earth. In this country many judges are not interpreting the laws, but are making the laws based on human moral standards, instead of God's values. Many judges even push God outside the Court Houses so they can judge according to their human wisdom.

Jehoshaphat also ordered the Levites, priests and heads of Israelite families to serve faithfully and wholeheartedly in the fear of the LORD and to warn people not to sin against the LORD. By so doing Jehoshaphat fulfilled the duty of an anointed king. He appointed leaders to assist him to rule over God's people, and he gave them clear instructions of their spiritual responsibility. Natural skills alone are helpful, but with the fear of the Lord, they are more powerful.

After this the Moabites and the Ammonites with some of the Meunites came to make war on Jehoshaphat. There was no way for him to win. But, "God will have a way when there seems to be no way" as one contemporary song says. In this case a carnal man will surrender, and a spiritual man will seek help from above.

> *"I lift up my eyes to the hills—*
> *where does my help come from?*
> *My help comes from the LORD,*
> *the Maker of heaven and earth."*
> (Psalm 121:1–2)

"Alarmed, Jehoshaphat resolved to inquire of the LORD, and he proclaimed a fast for all Judah" (2 Chronicles 20:3).

Through the prophet Jahaziel God answered his prayer, *"Do not be afraid or discouraged because of this vast army. For the battle is not yours, but God's"* (2 Chronicles 20.15).

Jehoshaphat fell down in worship before the Lord. Then some Levites stood up and praised the LORD, the God of Israel, with very loud voice. *"Early in the morning they left for the Desert of Tekoa. As they set out, Jehoshaphat stood and said, 'Listen to me, Judah and people of Jerusalem! Have faith in the LORD your God and you will be upheld; have faith in his prophets and you will be successful"* (vs. 20).

As they sang praises, the Lord defeated their enemies. They returned joyfully to Jerusalem, for the LORD had given them cause to rejoice. *"Later, Jehoshaphat king of Judah made an alliance with Ahaziah king of Israel, who was guilty of wickedness"* (vs. 35). They partnered with each other to build a fleet of trading ships. But, *"The ships were wrecked and were not able to set sail to trade"* (vs. 37).

If the saying "You win some, you lose some" is true in sports, and it is also true in the spiritual realm. Jehoshaphat was a great and spiritual king. But, he made the same mistake twice. The lesson I can draw from his life is that we need to be consistent in our walk with God in order to be constantly victorious. In the New Testament one of the keys to victorious life that the Lord Jesus teaches is, *"Abide in Me, and I in you. As the branch cannot bear fruit of itself, unless it abides in the vine, neither can you, unless you abide in Me"* (John 15:4—NKJV).

Josiah, healed by Jehovah, or Jehovah will support (640b.c.-608b.c.)

Josiah began to reign over Judah when he was eight years old, and he reigned for thirty-one years. The Bible says, *"He did what was right in the eyes of the LORD and walked in all the ways of his father David, not turning aside to the right or to the left"* (2 Kings 22:2). Hilkiah the high priest had some influence on the spiritual king. A great and needed revival came to the nation:

1. The temple was repaired. Three times in the Book of Genesis Abram built an altar to the Lord and called on the name of the Lord. His son Isaac built an altar to the Lord at Beersheba and also called on the name of the Lord (Genesis 26:25). Jacob came to Paddam Aram; there he built an altar to the Lord. To a spiritual man and woman the temple or the service of the Lord should be their first priority.
2. When the temple was being repaired Hilkiah found the Book of the Law in the temple. And Saphan the secretary read from it.
3. The words of the Book of the Law convicted of sin. Josiah inquired of the Lord, and He answered him through the prophetess Huldah:

"I am going to bring disaster on this place and its people, because they have forsaken me and burned incense to other gods and provoked me to anger by all the idols their hands have made, my anger will burn against this place and will not be quenched."

(2 Kings 22: 16–17)

However, because the heart of Josiah was right before the Lord, his eyes did not see all the disaster the Lord was going to bring on his nation.

4. At the order of the king all the articles made for Baal and Asherah and all the starry hosts were removed from the temple of the Lord. He tore down the

quarters of male shrine prostitutes. The Passover was re-instituted. Many other reformations took place before Josiah was slain by Pharaoh-neco, king of Egypt.

Ahab (874 b.c.—854 b.c.)

In the Southern kingdom there were eight good kings out of twenty kings. We have studied three of them. We're going to study one bad king of the Northern Kingdom. We know that all nineteen kings of the Northern Kingdom or Israel were bad kings. Ahab son of Omri was the worst of all because he "*did more evil in the eyes of the LORD than any of those before him*" (1 Kings 16:30). To him, the means justified the end. To strengthen the kingdom he took evil measures. To strengthen the economy he "*renewed the old relations with the Phoenicians and cemented them by his marriage with Jezebel, daughter of Ethbaal, king of Tyre.*" [24] Marrying the daughter of Ethbaal, king of Tyre for political reasons was normal. But that marriage relationship was considered as evil because it invited the Phoenician religion of Baal worship.

"*He set up an altar for Baal in the temple of Baal that he built in Samaria. Ahab also made an Asherah pole and did more to provoke the LORD, the God of Israel, to anger than did all the kings of Israel before him*" (1 Kings.16:32–33).

Jezebel was the patron of the prophets of Baal. "*At her instigation the altars of Yahweh were torn down. She inaugurated the first great religious persecution of the church, killing off the prophets of Yahweh with the sword.*"[25]

Many religions claim to worship God, but their god is not like the God of the Bible who is gracious. He granted Ahab an opportunity to turn to Him by giving Ahab victory over the Syrians. However, he failed to obey the Lord by sparing Benhadad.

The judgment of God was pronounced on Ahab, *"This is what the LORD says: 'You have set free a man I had determined should die. Therefore it is your life for his life, your people for his people.'"* (1 Kings 20:42)

Jezebel planned to destroy the religion of Yahweh root and branch and put that of Baal in its place. In this Ahab did not oppose her. [26] He did not also oppose her killing Naboth and taking his property.

God sent Elijah to meet Ahab and pronounced judgment on him. Also judgment was pronounced upon the line of Ahab and upon the line of Jezebel. God delayed judgment when Ahab repented in a measure, but did not revoke the sentence upon Ahab and Jezebel.

For three years there was no war between Israel and Aram. But in the third year the king of Israel allied with Jehoshaphat king of Judah to go fight against Ramoth Gilead. The prophets of Baal had told Ahab, *"Go, for the Lord will give it into the king's hand"* (1 Kings 22:6b). The king of Judah who had spiritual discernment asked that a prophet be called (1 Kings 22:5, 7). Micaiah, a prophet of God was called. And because he did not agree with the prophets of Baal, and pronounced bad news, Ahab ordered him to be kept in prison.

The prophecy of Elijah was fulfilled, *"So the king died and was brought to Samaria, and they buried him there. [38] They washed the chariot at a pool in Samaria (where the prostitutes bathed), and the dogs licked up his blood, as the word of the LORD had declared"* (1 Kings 22:37, 38).

There were a few good kings in Judah; they loved God and wished to obey Him. However none was perfect. They failed one way or the other. The Scripture tells us, *"Do not bring your servant into judgment, for no one living is righteous before you"* (Psalm

143:2). We should be thankful to God who does not spare His one and only Son so that we may be justified by His death.

Isaiah, Yesha yahu, "the salvation of Jehovah" or "Yaweh is salvation"

From the parable of the tenants recorded in Mark 12 and Matthew 21 we have learned that the office of the prophet is a challenging one. They are not popular. They are consulted when people have problems, but people don't want to listen to them because they say what people don't want to hear. On the contrary, people would listen to false prophets. I'd follow King David who consistently did not dare to touch God's anointed. But, I would say that a "mega Church" might not be a good Church if the preacher tickles the ears of the congregation rather than boldly pronouncing God's word.

Isaiah 6 records the personal call of the prophet when he saw a vision of the Lord sitting on the throne. After a person has experienced the glory of the Lord, who would not do what He asks him to do?

God spoke to Jeremiah, *"Before I formed you in the womb I knew you, before you were born I set you apart; I appointed you as a prophet to the nations"* (Jeremiah 1:5). I believe that the Lord also appointed Isaiah, but He let Isaiah volunteer, *"Here I am, send me."* The prophet just did what he was called to do. He condemned the arrogant (Isaiah 2:11–19), the priority of Judah to get rich (3:16–26).

Isaiah's message was not only "doom and gloom," but also hope during the reign of Manasseh king of Judah when the Baal worship was re-established, the weak were oppressed, the just were persecuted.

Isaiah prophesied to many kings regarding judgment and salvation to Judah and to other nations (Isaiah 13–27). Isaiah is best known for his prophecy on the Messiah who would be a king and at the same time a servant. The prophet fully realized the holiness of God for he was transformed when he saw the vision of God.

His message was about God's power to save people from sin and the kings from political powers. He called all nations to trust in God because there is no other God. God will establish His eternal kingdom.

Isaiah called the people of Judah, who had been miserably defeated, to repent, to do right, and to stop their meaningless sacrifices in the temple (Isaiah 1:1–20).

Isaiah was a great prophet not because of his gift of oratory, not because of his gift of expressing by illustrations (the vineyard in chapter 5), or by metaphor (leaders of Sodom representing the kings of Judah), but because he was God's spokesman. His message and that of other prophets are the inspired Word of God, and are to be obeyed *"For prophecy never had its origin in the will of man, but men spoke from God as they were carried along by the Holy Spirit"* (2 Peter 1:21).

Isaiah has been called the fifth evangelist, and his book, the fifth gospel because Isaiah and the New Testament present the Lord Jesus as their common theme. Isaiah prophesied the life, the death, the resurrection and the second coming of Christ with definiteness and clarity (cf. Luke 4:16–22 with Isaiah 61:1–4).

As the true man of God many of his prophecies such as the one concerning the king of Assyria (37:33) were fulfilled. There are other prophecies which were not fulfilled in his lifetime, but they stand fulfilled today. For instance, the prophecy concerning the city of Babylon, *"And Babylon, the glory of kingdoms, the beauty of the Chaldeans' excellency, shall be as when God overthrew Sodom and Gomorrah. It shall never be inhabited, neither shall it be dwelt in from generation to generation"* (13:19). Archeology has revealed the accuracy of this prophecy.

We could write a five hundred-page book about this great prophet, and many Bible scholars have done so. Above are a few things Isaiah has done for me. We know that God gives to some five talents, to others three talents or one. Our part is to be wise stewards of His talents. I believe we will receive the same reward if we bring back to the Giver the same return He has given to us, regardless of the number of talents we have gained.

Daniel, judgment of God, God my judge

People are born something, whether musician, athlete, or artist. Daniel was born an administrator, and prophet. For seventy years he served Babylon and the Medes when he was over eighty. Daniel was a successful man.

A Christian who would dedicate his/her life to serve the Lord will be really blessed to hear God saying, "Ye good and faithful servant." Here is God's estimate of Daniel, "O Daniel, a man greatly beloved" (Daniel 10:11). That is the commendation I would like to hear from the Lord. The Bible speaks of different crowns as rewards to those who faithfully serve God. I will be happy with two words from Him, "Good job!"

Daniel was "greatly beloved" because of his purpose, his prayer and his prophecy.

As a man of purpose Daniel resolved not to defile himself with the royal food and wine. In other words he determined not to be defiled by the immorality of paganism. Christians are in the world, but not of the world.

As a man of prayer Daniel would not make any decision without inquiring first of the Lord. When he was facing imminent death Daniel asked his friends to join him in prayer, *"He urged them to plead for mercy from the God of heaven concerning this mystery, so that he and his friends might not be executed with the rest of the wise men of Babylon*" (Daniel 2:17). Under Darius three administrators and under them 120 satraps were appointed to rule throughout the kingdom. Daniel was one of the administrators, and because God was with him, "*Now Daniel so distinguished himself among the administrators and the satraps by his exceptional qualities that the king planned to set him over the whole kingdom*" (6:3). That caused the other officials to become jealous of Daniel, and they petitioned the king to issue a decree to ban all prayers offered to any gods for a period of thirty days. But, Daniel feared God rather than man, "*Now when Daniel learned that the decree had been published, he went home to his upstairs room where the windows opened toward Jerusalem. Three times a day he got down on his knees and prayed, giving thanks to his God, just as he had done before*" (6:10). His courage came from his trust in the Lord for he knew that the Redeemer would save him, "*I call to the LORD, who is worthy of praise, and I am saved from my enemies*" (Psalm 18:3).

In the Ancient Times the king's decrees were strictly enforced. Even though Daniel was the king's favorite top official; the king could not spare his life. Daniel was thrown into the lions' den. But the Lord sent His angels to shut the mouths of the lions.

God saved His servant, and judged His servant's enemies. Those who falsely accused Daniel along with their families were thrown into the lion's den, and then no angels shut the mouth of the lions.

Persecutions and snares strengthen the faith of godly people. Believers came out victorious after they had passed the test, "*So Daniel prospered during the reign of Darius and the reign of Cyrus the Persian*" (6:28).

From his book we know that Daniel was knowledgeable of God's word. He knew that according to the prophet Jeremiah the desolation of Jerusalem would last for seventy years. So he *"turned to the Lord God and pleaded with him in prayer and petition, in fasting, and in sackcloth and ashes"* (9:3). Daniel is the model of "prayer without ceasing."

Daniel prayed when his life was in danger. He prayed when he received insight of the Word of God. Daniel 10 records the fourth time he prayed when he was given a revelation concerning a great war. At that time he fasted, he mourned for three weeks. After the three weeks were over Daniel saw a "Christophany," or the appearance of the pre-incarnate Jesus.

Moses asked the Lord to let him see God's glory. But he only saw God's back. As for Daniel who was highly esteemed, he saw the Lord Jesus before the Lord transfigured in front of the three disciples. And the Lord Jesus told him that Daniel's prayers were considered, but the answers sometime seemed delayed because there is spiritual warfare going on that our natural eyes cannot see.

3) Daniel was a man of prophecy
Our Lord labeled him, "Daniel the prophet" (Matthew 24:15). His prophecies were concerned with the Gentile nations. This does not imply that the Book of Daniel was not written for the nation of Israel. This book is of the universal sovereignty of God, and shows that He overrules the idolatry and intolerance of the Gentiles. In the Olivet Discourse our Lord quoted from the Book of Daniel. The Book of Daniel unlocked the enigma of the Book of Revelation. Daniel's account amplifies and clarifies Paul's revelation concerning "the man of sin."

Each of us is unique. The Lord creates us not like Daniel. But Daniel was great mainly because he was in unison with God. He knew what God's will was for him. He lived a victorious life in the natural and in the spiritual. That is the life our Lord intends for all of His children, "*The thief comes only to steal and kill and destroy; I have come that they may have life, and have it to the full*" (John 10:10).

11

In Christ

$\mathcal{I}$n the Book of Mark we read that the Lord Jesus rebuked the deaf and mute spirit which possessed a boy, "*I command you, come out of him and never enter him again*" (Mark 9:25). When Jesus had gone indoors, his disciples asked him why they couldn't drive it out. The Lord, replied, "*This kind can come out only by prayer*" (vs. 29).

The Lord teaches us that we can overcome an evil spirit only after we ask Him for spiritual power. Spirit is not physical, and cannot be subdued by human natural strength, but by divine power. That power is available to the believers of Christ. What we need to do is to enter in the Holy of Holies, and ask him to empower us to cast out the demon.

The Lord Jesus told his disciples, "*I tell you the truth, and anyone who has faith in me will do what I have been doing. He will do even greater things than these, because I am going to the Father*" (John 14: 12). How can we do greater things than He did? We can if He strengthens us, and if we ask Him for His super power. If we do not live in His constant presence we cannot draw upon His unlimited resource. If we can only tap in His resource, we can do greater things.

The best counsel a pastor or a counselor can give to a person is to advice that one gets connected with God. That thought agrees with Jesus' teaching, *"Apart from me you can do nothing."* An abundant life is a life "in Christ."

One morning a forty-year-old man called me, and said, "Uncle An, I need to talk to you. I can't stand it; I do not feel at ease. I do not love my wife any more."

I've known this man for almost twenty years. When he came to this country the church helped his family settle in Olympia, Washington. The pastor, my wife and I witnessed to his family about Christ. He got saved, and we studied the Bible with him and his wife.

One night, long after they accepted the Lord, the man was angry with his wife and he got violent with her. She called the police, and he was thrown in jail, but she bailed him out. Then he got angry with the pastor because he did not take sides with him. They stopped going to the church after that incident.

Fifteen years passed; he called me. I invited him to come over my home to see me. Even though I'm not a marriage counselor, I told him what the Bible tells a husband to do, *"Husbands, love your wives, just as Christ loved the church and gave himself up for her"* (Ephesians 5:25–26). I also suggested that he needed to pray. He left my home and went to work.

The next morning I called him to follow up on his situation. He told me he felt fine, and things were back to normal. He said that he felt better after he prayed.

In Christ we have that power to, *"Be kind and compassionate to one another, forgiving each other, just as in Christ God forgave you"*

(Ephesians 4:32). In Christ we can conquer our "me first" mentality. Then, we can enjoy an abundant life in Christ.

I have another success story to share with you. Loc is his name. My wife and I met him in a convalescence center. He stayed there for a short time to recuperate his strength after an open-heart surgery. We talked to him, shared the Lord with him, and gave him some Christian reading materials. He took time to listen to us and discussed spiritual matters with us. However, he decided not to receive Jesus Christ as Lord and Savior. We kept in touch with him, and became friends. He always showed his appreciation to us.

Last week Loc was rushed into the hospital due to an acute headache he could not bear. His brain was bleeding. His Doctor had to drain the blood out and give him some medication to ease his pain. When we heard the news, we went in the hospital to see him, and to pray for him. I did not have enough faith to think that he would come out alive.

But, by the mercy of God, the next day, he stopped bleeding, and his health was improved.

The point is that the privileges of Christians are the ability to have access to the Son's power. We can't do anything for Loc but to ask God to release His healing power to heal that old man. Through our concerns, Loc saw the love of Christ, and His love has the power to give Loc faith in the Savior.

When we are in Christ we will live "in the Name of Jesus." The apostle Paul teaches, *"And whatever you do, whether in word or deed, do it all in the name of the Lord Jesus, giving thanks to God the Father through him"* (Colossians 3:17). Living in Jesus' Name means to walk with His Spirit, and to do what brings Him glory.

A member of the Church asked the late Pastor J. Vernon McGee, "May I go to a bar?" Pastor McGee replied, "That depends on what you do there. I could." Yes, we may go to the bar to share our testimonies, and to tell people how the Lord is gracious to us and that He has delivered us from sin.

Temptation

There are diverse kinds of faith: saving faith, living faith, working faith. The living faith delivers the believer from the power of sin.

Temptation is not a little matter in the lives of the believers. This issue was dated back to the Garden of Eden. Satan tempted Eve due to jealousy. Before God created Adam, Satan was trusted with the dominion over God's creation. After his rebellion against the Lord, that privilege was taken away from him. Therefore, Satan was angry against the Lord, and since he could not do anything to God, he tempted man to sin like him. And he was successful.

Satan knows that when believers sin they cannot communicate with their Lord, and will join his company. The Bible calls it the scheme of the devil. When a Christian gives in to temptation he is "devoured" by the "lion." Unfortunately, many of God's people neither know the scheme of the devil, nor have enough power to resist temptation.

What is the difference between the First Man Adam and the Second Man Jesus? The First Man failed because he faced temptation on his own strength, at his own will. The Second Man Jesus took the test with the power of Holy Spirit.

To overcome temptation a Christian needs: (1) to store the experiences of Adam and of Christ somewhere in his memory; (2) to be alert, and be able to differentiate between trial and temptation; and (3) to use Christ's techniques to deal with temptation.

For most of Christians the best way to deal with temptation is to run. The following would be a good illustration. An alcoholic was invited to an AA (Alcoholics Anonymous) meeting. He was warned that on his way to the meeting, signs showing bottles of whiskey would tempt him. He was instructed to run, and not to look at those signs. The man made it to the meeting. That is a great technique; there is a better way, and that is to be in Christ, to stay close to Him. Jesus Christ claims, "I have overcome the world." We can trust His word. In Him nothing is impossible.

The Lord Jesus in His divine nature could have easily defeated the devil in the wilderness. Yet, He chose to rely on the word of God as His defense. By so doing He decided to defeat Satan in His humanity, so that His followers would have the same pattern and battle plan to win our spiritual warfare.

Peace with God

I was born in Viet Nam, and grew up during wartime, from World War II through the Liberation War against France's domination, to the civil war between the North and the South. In his book *"The Fourth Dimension"* Pastor Yonggi Cho shared that Korea has had five thousand years of wars. Many other countries have experienced the same curses as Viet Nam and Korea. The Bible has given us an answer. Wars, disasters, and sufferings entered the world when the first man Adam disobeyed his Creator.

Among different names, the Lord Jesus is called "the Prince of Peace." We are startled to hear Him declare:

> *"Do you think I came to bring peace on earth? No, I tell you, but division. From now on there will be five in one family divided against each other, three against two and two against three. They will be divided, father against son and son against father, mother against daughter and daughter against mother, mother-in-law against daughter-in-law and daughter-in-law against mother-in-law."*
>
> (Luke 12:51–53)

Some people say, "No Jesus, no peace." That statement supports the Lord Jesus' claim, "*I am the way and the truth and the life, no one comes to the Father except through me."* (John 14:6). The peace He brings to this world is the peace with God. It is the primary peace, the ultimate peace. If one does not have peace with God he cannot have peace with men. A person who claims to believe God but hates people, is a liar, *"Whoever does not love does not know God, because God is love"* (1 John 4:8).

That is the peace that our Lord speaks of, *"Peace I leave with you; my peace I give you. I do not give to you as the world gives. Do not let your hearts be troubled and do not be afraid"* (John 14:27). That is the kind of peace that transcends all understanding. If we don't take the peace the Lord Jesus offers, we will never have inner peace with ourselves, or outer peace with the world.

That explains why God required His Only Begotten Son to die on the cross. That is the only way He could bring humankind back to Him.

If so, will we ever literally see peace on earth? The Bible teaches that the Lord Jesus was born of the Virgin Mary; He died for our sins, He rose again, and He will come back to establish a thousand years of peace. There will be no war after His Second Coming.

In the meantime, we may enjoy the inner peace, and peace with our families, with our relatives, and with our neighbors when we receive Jesus Christ as Lord and Savior. When we are waiting for His Second Coming, His kingdom and His lordship reside in us, and we can enjoy a perfect peace.

This book has been written to share with believers the ideas on how to enjoy an "abundant life." If you happen to read this book quite by chance, that's God's will for you to have peace with Him, by accepting the Lord Jesus to come into your heart as Lord and Savior. That's the first step to beginning a new quality life in

Christ Jesus. Just say, "Yes" to Him, and you will never regret, and you will never want to let Him go.

Peace is what we need in our daily life. Peace can only be found in the Lord Jesus who is the Prince of Peace. People are running around looking for peace. In church people greet each other, "Peace be with you," and not many experience peace. They are still caught up in fighting the wrong enemies, quarreling with their husbands or their wives. In order to live a peaceful life we need to believe His word, *"Peace I leave with you; my peace I give you. I do not give to you as the world gives. Do not let your hearts be troubled and do not be afraid"* (John 14:27). If we hide His word in our hearts we will not sin. We can conquer depression, anxiety or related mental sicknesses when we store His peace in our hearts. Practice to be in fellowship with the Lord may help to keep that sense of peace. When His kingdom is in us, His mighty power will dispel all apprehensions.

Faith

W. Graham Scroggie said, "Behind the Book was a Person. In the Old Testament He was predicted; in the Gospel He was present; in the Acts He was proclaimed; in the Epistles He was possessed; and in the Apocalypse (Revelation) He is predominant." So, the Lord Jesus is the central hero of the Book, and God's plan of salvation is the main theme of the Book.

The apostle John stated the purpose of his Gospel, *"But these are written that you may believe that Jesus is the Christ, the Son of God, and that by believing you may have life in his name"* (John 20:31). We may apply that statement to the purpose of the whole Bible that is God's plan of salvation. Because God is love, He does not *"want anyone to perish, but everyone to come to repentance"*

(2 Peter 3:9). For thousand of years God patiently revealed His plan of salvation.

The apostle John wrote his Gospel so the readers may believe in Jesus' name, and that faith saves them not only from sins, but also from various sorts of troubles.

We can agree with Peale that we can find in the Bible the most powerful force. That force is God's power that he wishes to give to His children, to help them in living a successful life. We can learn to think positively, to have faith, to be confident, and to be able to do many good things for the Lord and for ourselves.

"The righteous shall live by faith" is a good principle from the Old Testament time and in the New Testament time. Hebrews 11 gives us a list of the heroes of faith. We should follow their examples, for faith has the power to sustain us, to take us through trials and tribulations. Without faith one cannot please God, and cannot live an abundant life.

Prayer

Many religions claim they worship God, and do not know the Bible. Their gods must be different than the God of Abraham, of Isaac, and of Jacob. Christians worship the God of the patriarchs who reveals himself through the Bible. He is personal. The Bible affirms that God hears when we speak to Him, and we may communicate with Him. There are different reasons why people pray. Abraham interceded for Abimelech, his wife, and his slave girls. Abraham also pleaded on behalf of Sodom and Gomorrah. A noteworthy fact is that prayer is not mentioned before the time of Abraham. After him, his servant Eliezer of Damascus prayed that the Lord would show him the right bride for Isaac. And throughout the Bible we see people prayed, and prayed, and prayed.

I found the narrative recorded in Luke 9:28–42 quite interesting in regard to the power of prayer. Eight days after Peter confessed, "You are Christ, the Son of the Living God," and after the Lord foretold His death and His resurrection, He took Peter, James and John to a prayer meeting that was on the mountain. The Bible tells us, *"As he was praying, the appearance of his face changed, and his clothes became as bright as a flash of lightning"* (Luke 9:29).

The Old Testament (Exodus 34) recorded another circumstance similar to the Transfiguration of our Lord that we will study afterward.

Luke asserts that the Lord's face changed as he was praying, and His clothes became as a flash of lightning, in other words He was metamorphosed into a different being. His prayer actually transformed Him. When He prayed He entered into the Holy of Holies, He was in the awesome presence of the Almighty. God sent Moses and Elijah to talk with the Lord Jesus. They appeared in glorious splendor. After they had left the company, a cloud appeared and enveloped our Lord and his three disciples. And God validated Jesus' claim, *"This is my Son, whom I have chosen; listen to him"* (Luke 9:35). That meant all the authority in heaven and on the earth had been given to Jesus Christ. He got access to the titanic resource that would help Him to do what He needed to do.

The Holy Spirit must have revealed to Nicodemus the truth when he acknowledged, *"Rabbi, we know you are a teacher who has come from God. For no one could perform the miraculous signs you are doing if God were not with him"* (John 3:2).

In the New Testament, the Book of Mark indicates, *"Very early in the morning, while it was still dark, Jesus got up, left the house and went off to a solitary place, where he prayed"* (Mark 1:35). The Lord got up early and prayed because he knew that he would travel throughout Galilee, preaching in their synagogues and driving out demons. Without prayer the Lord could not have energy for traveling, teaching, preaching, healing, and performing miracles.

We do not know how the Lord Jesus prayed, but we know that his prayer was powerful and effective, so we may say that He prayed earnestly and in faith. What effect did Jesus' prayer have on His ministry?

1. He became the One on demand; people need Him (Luke 9:37). A man in the crowd was desperate, but he knew that the Lord Jesus could help him (vss. 38–40).
2. The Lord Jesus had spent time with God the Father. He was confident of His ability because He was aware of the power of the Father that was available to Him (vss. 41–43).
3. Working miracles was only a part of the Lord Jesus' ministry. Prayer kept Him in focus on His main purpose (vs. 44). He knew God's will through prayer.
4. Prayer resulted in Jesus' great teaching (vss. 46–50).

We can draw some lessons from the above conclusions. First, we pray to be charged up for service. The Lord Jesus states, *"You did not choose me, but I chose you and appointed you to go and bear fruit—fruit that will last. Then the Father will give you whatever you ask in my name"* (John 15:16). We pray to be filled with the Holy Spirit in order to have great power to serve the Lord God and the Lord Jesus, not to be holier than others. Luke recorded the Lord's promise, *"But you will receive power when the Holy Spirit comes on you; and you will be my witnesses in Jerusalem, and in all Judea and Samaria, and to the ends of the earth"* (Acts 1:8). The power of the Holy Spirit was given to the disciples on the Day of Pentecost, and is available to all born again Christians today to empower them to bear fruit, and to bring glory to His Name, Name above all Name.

Second, prayer strengthens our faith, and bolsters our confidence in our ability. We know that the apostle Paul was a prayer warrior because he used the phrase "I pray that . . ." in his epistles to the Christians in Rome, to the Christians in Ephesus and to Philemon. That is why he can say, "*I can do all things through Christ who strengthens me*" (Philippians 4:13—NKJ). We too, we can do nothing without fervent prayer, a kind of prayer that connects us to the source of power. We are talking about political power. Even the President of the United States does not have that kind of power if he does not rely on the Lord for wisdom and energy. An atheist who objects the President's prayer on his inauguration, "Please help me God," does not understand how critical that short prayer is. A leader who seeks help from above will not likely kill any atheist who doesn't agree with his policy.

Third, prayer keeps us in focus. Because the apostle Paul prays he can state, "*But one thing I do.*" He would not let anything interfere with his "one thing," but, rather he "*press toward the goal for the prize of the upward call of God in Christ Jesus*" (Philippians 3:14—NKJV).

Fourth, our Lord chose us to bear fruit—fruit that will last. To bear fruit, we must abide in Him, because, without Him we can do nothing. To abide in Him, we must plug into His power source. Prayer connects us to that unlimited source. That power source will enable us to do more than what we alone can do, to love more than what we can love.

Matthew 26 gives us an account of the Lord Jesus' last hours He spent with His own. They retreated to a place called Gethsemane. There He asked the disciples to sit in one place while He went to another place to pray. He took with Him Peter, James and

John, and asked them, *"remain here and keep watch with me."* But they couldn't because, *"the spirit is willing, but the flesh is weak."*

But the Lord Jesus had no other choice; He must pray because the hour had come for the Son of Man to be betrayed into the hands of men. He had to pray to be strengthened to suffer on the cross.

Jesus must have gotten up early in the morning for His daily devotion. That day He did God's business. By the time He arrived at the Garden of Gethsemane, He and His disciples were so tired that they could not watch with Him for even an hour. Then He was taken to the high priest, to the council, and to Pontius Pilate the governor. So, he went twenty-four hours without rest.

His morning prayer and His evening prayer were required even for the Messiah to go through all of His sufferings.

The Lord Jesus set for us an example of prayer. Unless we are idle, if we are busy for the Lord's work we must take time to pray. If we feel weary, if we feel exhausted, I think that it's time to pray.

"Ask and it will be given to you; seek and you will find; knock and the door will be opened to you" (Luke 11:9).

1) Ask

Why do we need to ask? Does God know everything? Yes, He knows what we need, the Bible says. We ask for permission to use His resource. He is not our storekeeper, or our agent whom we ask to do things for us, but rather we must ask for the tool we need to do the job. Our Heavenly Father is the Owner of all the power in the universe. When we lack of wisdom, ask Him for it. When we need healing, ask Him for the healing power, and it will be given to us.

How do we ask? At the beginning of Luke 11, the Lord Jesus has given an illustration of what he states in verse 9. In that example He indicates that if we are persistent enough we can get what we ask even at midnight.

In Luke 18 the Lord tells another story about a judge who neither feared God, nor cared about men. *"And there was a widow in that town who kept coming to him with the plea, 'Grant me justice against my adversary"*(Luke 18:3). However, because the widow kept bothering him, finally he granted her request. *"When you ask, you do not receive, because you ask with wrong motives, that you may spend what you get on your pleasures"* (James 4:3).

One day when the Lord Jesus was teaching, a man from the crowd asked the Lord to tell his brother to give him his share of the inheritance. The Lord told him that was a wrong prayer because the Lord is not a judge over human disputes.

Chapter 10 of the Book of Mark recorded the story of the Zebedee brothers, James and John who made a request to the Lord, *"Let one of us sit at your right and the other at your left in your glory"* (Mark 10:37). The ten other disciples who heard them became indignant with James and John. We may feel the same today, but, who knows, many Christians today may ask with wrong motives.

In his second epistle to the Corinthians the apostle Paul told us that he was given a thorn in the flesh which he called "a messenger of Satan," to torment him. Three times Paul asked the Lord to take it away from him, but the Lord replied, *"My grace is sufficient for you, for my power is made perfect in weakness"* (2 Corinthians 12:9). Even though Paul did not ask God with wrong motives, the answer was "No." And Paul was happy with the answer, because God's power is perfect. What more can we ask? His grace and His power are all we need.

2) Seek

Suppose I receive a telephone call from a stranger asking me to send him one thousand dollars for paying his bills. I would ask him, "Who are you? I don't know you." On the other hand, if my natural son, who is not living at home, calls me from any part of the world, and asks for some money, I would try my best to provide for him.

The Lord Jesus teaches, *"But seek first his kingdom and his righteousness, and all these things will be given to you as well"* (Matthew 6:33–34). Before asking God for a favor we must seek His face, so that we are not stranger, but His own.

3) Knock

Any children may knock at the door of their parents, and it would be opened for them. Their parents then ask them, "What do you need, son or honey? What can we do for you?"

Since the Lord already gives us permission, we may knock, ask, seek, and believe that *"He shall supply all our needs according to the riches of His glory."*

When we pray, we know that we may ask for anything in His name, and we will receive it (John 14:14). The apostle James concurs with our Lord when he says, *"You do not have because you do not ask God"* (James 4:2 b).

Worship

King David rejoiced with those who said to him, "Let us go to the house of the LORD" to worship God.

One of the reasons we believe in God is that each of us has a spiritual need. It is to worship someone or something. For instance, a pantheist believes that God and the universe are identical, and he worships all gods.[27] Christians believe Three Persons of the Godhead or Trinity, and worship God the Father, God the Son, and God the Holy Spirit. God alone is worthy to be worshipped as the Psalter states, *"For who in the skies above can compare with the LORD? Who is like the LORD among the heavenly beings"* (Psalm 89:6).

Allan and Borror confirm, "Worship is an active response to God whereby we declare his worth . . . Worship is not just a feeling; it is a declaration." (Worship, page 16) Pastor Ralph Martin concurs, "To worship God is to ascribe to Him supreme worth, for He alone is worthy" [28]

Therefore, when we worship a person, no matter how great he is, we violate God's commandment, *"You shall have no other gods before me"* (Deuteronomy 5:7). How do we worship? Dr. Segler answers, "Worship is more than conversation; it is also encounter. In this encounter, God confronts man and makes demands upon him"[29]

In answering the question, "What is the greatest commandment?" our Lord quotes Deuteronomy 6:5, "Love the LORD your God with all your heart and with all your soul and with all your strength". The apostle Paul clarified that the spiritual act of worship is complete when we offer our whole bodies as living sacrifices, *"Therefore, I urge you, brothers, in view of God's mercy, to offer your bodies as living sacrifices, holy and pleasing to God—this is your spiritual act of worship"* (Romans 12:1). Warren W. Wiersbe puts it this way, "Worship is the believer's response of all that he is-- mind, emotion, will, and body—to all that God is and says and does. This response has its mystical side in objective obedience to God's revealed truth. It is a loving response that is balanced by the fear of the Lord, and it is a deepening response as the believer comes to know God better."[30]

Pastor Perry F. Webb believes that true worship results in stronger faith, brighter hope, deeper love, broadened sympathies, purer heart, and [a] more resolute will to do the will of God.

In Harmony With God

Second Chronicles 20 gives us an account of victory resulting from true worship.

In 870 B. C. King Asa of Judah died and rested with his fathers, Jehoshaphat his son succeeded him as king. The first two kings of Judah, Rehoboam and Abijam, did not measure up to God's standard. 2 Chronicles 14 tells us, *"Asa did what was good and right in the eyes of the LORD his God"* (vs. 2).

The saying, "Like father, like son" may not be always true. But it was in the case of Jehoshaphat, *"The LORD was with Jehoshaphat because in his early years he walked in the ways his father David had followed. He did not consult the Baals but sought the God of his father and followed his commands rather than the practices of Israel"* (17:3, 4).

One time, *"the Moabites and Ammonites with some of the Meunites came to make war on Jehoshaphat"* (20:1). The enemies outnumbered the army of Judah. In a case like this, any Commander-in-Chief has two options: either to surrender, or to run for his life. Jehoshaphat had another option: that was to cry out to God, believing that the Lord would hear him and deliver him from his enemies. The king acknowledged God, recited God's help in the past, admitted his weakness, and expressed his trust in the Lord.

During the 2004 General Election in the US, a poll showed that a majority—maybe over 70% of the people—wanted a believing President. What would have happened to Judah if Jehoshaphat had not walked in the ways of David, and if the king did not seek the God of his father? The spirituality of a king or of a president makes a difference to himself and to his people.

The wisdom of Jehoshaphat came from the fear of the Lord. The Lord answered his prayer, *"Do not be afraid or discouraged because of this vast army for the battle is not yours, but God's"* (20:15b). Jehoshaphat and his army did not have to fight, they just [30]needed to sing praise to the Lord. *"As they began to sing and praise, the LORD set ambushes against the men of Ammon and Moab and Mount Seir who were invading Judah, and they were defeated"* (vs. 22). *"And the kingdom of Jehoshaphat was at peace, for his God had given him rest on every side"* (vs. 30).

Meditation on His Word

Through the failure of Adam and the victory of our Lord, we have learned that we can win the spiritual battles by correctly handling God's word. Head knowledge will not do us good. One Psalter wrote, *"I have hidden your word in my heart that I might not sin against you"* (Psalm 119:11).

It's more comfortable to live a mediocre life. But, to enjoy a victorious Christian life we need to invest our time in the studying of the word. In business we need capital, time and effort to make money. The same principle works in God's business.

In this country people are very afraid of the influenza epidemic. In the fall of the year 2004 due to some technical error, the supply of flu shots did not meet the demands of the concerned citizens. So, people were almost in panic. Many, including my wife had to wait in line for hours to get a shot.

We will not be immune from a sin disease if we do not have a dose of the Word in our heart. We need to speak it, to meditate on it day and night, and to let it sink deep into our subconscious. The more we study the Word, the more we are fed on the Word, and the better we are equipped to fight the good fight.

Obedience

Adam and Eve did die physically and spiritually because they were not in harmony with God. They listened to the serpent rather to their Creator. Christians, more than one time, opted to walk in the flesh, rather in the Spirit.

The Lord prefers obedience to sacrifices. He commanded King Saul to completely destroy the Amalekites, but the soldiers took sheep and cattle from the plunder. The Lord was not happy about their disobedience.

"Does the LORD delight in burnt offerings and sacrifices as much as in obeying the voice of the LORD ? To obey is better than sacrifice, and to heed is better than the fat of rams." (1 Samuel 15:22).

Our Lord agrees with God's word when He teaches, *"Blessed rather are those who hear the word of God and obey it"* (Luke 11:28). He does what He preaches; He obeys completely the Father, even when He has to die.

"And being found in appearance as a man, he humbled himself and became obedient to death—even death on a cross!" (Philippians 2:8).

The Lord Jesus, in the garden of Gethsemane, the night He was betrayed, He prayed, *"My Father, if it is not possible for this cup to be taken away unless I drink it, may your will be done"* (Matthew 26:42).

In the New Testament, in many instances, our Lord set many examples of complete obedience. To live a life committed to obedience, it costs us a lot. However, the reward is guaranteed according to the promise of our Lord. Two thousand years ago his inner circle was concerned about their reward. Peter asked Him, *"We have left everything to follow you! What then will there be for us"* (Matthew 19:27)? The Lord did not rebuke Peter for his interest in the reward. He made clear that our service to God will be recompensed, *"I tell you the truth, at the renewal of all things, when the Son of Man sits on his glorious throne, you who have followed me will also sit on twelve thrones, judging the twelve tribes of Israel"* (vs. 28).

Deuteronomy 28 provides God's children with two choices:

blessings and curses; blessings for obedience and curses for disobedience. If we fully obey the Lord our God and carefully follow all His commands we will be blessed wherever we go, and whatever we have will be blessed. On the contrary, if we do not fully obey the Lord our God, and follow all His commands and decrees, we will be cursed everywhere we go, and whatever we do will be cursed.

Is God a totalitarian? No. As a Vietnamese saying goes, "If fish is not marinated with salt it will be spoiled. With the same token, if a child disobeys his parents, he will be spoiled." God wants His children to be obedient to Him because His thoughts are higher than our thoughts, His way higher than our way. He knows the beginning and the end, and His plan is perfect. We'd better obey Him to live a life in abundance.

Obedience is the key to success for Christians. If we wish to be continuously in the presence of the Lord, we must submit our will to His will as our Lord claimed in the Garden of Gethsemane, "Not my will but thine be done."

EPILOGUE

"*If we go along with God's will, we will survive, if we go against God's will, we shall surely die.*" (Vietnamese proverb)

The above proverb is supported by many verses in the Old Testament. Following is one, "*The gracious hand of our God helps everyone who looks to him. But he becomes very angry with anyone who deserts him*" (Ezra 8:22b). Knowing God's will and doing His will is essential to humankind, regardless of the race.

In the Old Testament we read scriptures such as:

"*For the LORD knoweth the way of the righteous: but the way of the ungodly shall perish*" (Psalm 1:6).

"*Keep my commandments, and live; and my law as the apple of thine eye*" (Proverbs 7:1).

If we are in harmony with God, not only we survive, but we also succeed,

"*And he [31] shall be like a tree planted by the rivers of water, that bringeth forth his fruit in his season; his leaf also shall not wither; and whatsoever he doeth shall prosper*" (Psalm 1:3).

The Lord Jesus tells us that He came to give us life and life in abundance. His plan for us is that we prosper in this life and in the life to come. Christian life is not free from sufferings, difficulties, conflicts, and antagonists, but is a life filled with love, joy, and peace. It is free from sin, and from its fruits such as hate, anxiety, anger, and jealousy.

Our Lord asserts that when we live a victorious Christian life, God will be glorified, and we are truly Jesus' disciples.

"When you bear a lot of fruit, it brings glory to my Father. It shows that you are my disciples" (John 15:8).

This study has helped me to grow spiritually. I hope that it will draw you closer to God, and you will learn to walk in the Spirit, so that everything will go well with you.

"Dear friend, I pray that you may enjoy good health and that all may go well with you, even as your soul is getting along well" (3 John 2).

BIBLIOGRAPHY

Holy Bible, New International Version

Holy Bible, King James Version

Krysten Crawford, CNN/Money staff writer, March 4, 2005

VietBao Daily News, March 4, 2005

Mark Twain, *Adventures of Huckleberry Finn*

Scott M. Huse, *The Collapse of Evolution,* Baker Book House Company, 1986

Norman V. Peale, *The Power of Positive Thinking,* Random House, Inc. New York, 1994,

Wycliffe Bible Commentary, Electronic Database. Copyright (c) 1962 by Moody Press

Fausset's Bible Dictionary, Electronic Database Copyright (c)1998 by Biblesoft

International Standard Bible Encyclopaedia, Electronic Database Copyright (c)1996 by Biblesoft

Oxford English Dictionary

Endnotes

1. For simplification purposes, when the word "he" is used for a person, that implies a man and/or a woman.
2. Today we are facing many natural disasters such as flood, drought, and hurricanes because we fail to take care of God's creation. People call natural disasters, "acts of God," when they are actually "acts of people." While we should not overemphasize the importance of nature, we should learn how to manage the environment with care, if we want to preserve humankind.
3. In order to multiply, every species needs a male and a female. Two males or two females cannot reproduce.
4. The celebrity homemaker strolls the grounds of her New York home after her prison release Friday. March 4, 2005: 11:04 AM EST
    By Krysten Crawford, CNN/Money staff writer
5. Translated from the Vietnamese article
6. Scott M. Huse, The Collapse of Evolution, Baker Book House Company, 1986, page 30
7. Norman V. Peale, The Power of Positive Thinking, Random House, Inc. New York, 1994, p. 184
8. Id. p. 44

9   (from The Wycliffe Bible Commentary, Electronic Database. Copyright (c) 1962 by Moody Press)
10 Half a century ago, and maybe in this 21st Century in the Third World countries, poor people have rolled their own cigarettes.
11 J. Sidlow Baxter, Explore the Book, Zonderman Publishing House, Grand Rapids, Michigan, 1966, p. 25
12 From Nelson's Illustrated Bible Dictionary, Copyright (c) 1986, Thomas Nelson Publishers
13 From The Wycliffe Bible Commentary, Electronic Database. Copyright (c) 1962 by Moody Press.
14 Now the dry area southwest of the Dead Sea.
15 Some teachers of the Bible think Abram sold his wife.
16 From The Wycliffe Bible Commentary, Electronic Database. Copyright (c) 1962 by Moody Press.
17 From The Wycliffe Bible Commentary, Electronic Database. Copyright (c) 1962 by Moody Press.
18 It sounds like the Abrahamic covenant
19 (from Fausset's Bible Dictionary, Electronic Database Copyright (c)1998 by Biblesoft)
20 International Standard Bible Encyclopaedia, Electronic Database Copyright (c)1996 by Biblesoft
21 Ibid
22 Ibid
23 Ibid
24 (from International Standard Bible Encyclopaedia, Electronic Database Copyright (c)1996 by Biblesoft)
25 Ibid
26 Ibid
27 Oxford English Dictionary

28 Worship In the Early Church, p. 10
29 Christian Worship, p. 9
30 Real Worship p. 27
31 The righteous or the one who is in harmony with God.

listen|imagine|view|experience

AUDIO BOOK DOWNLOAD INCLUDED WITH THIS BOOK!

In your hands you hold a complete digital entertainment package. Besides purchasing the paper version of this book, this book includes a free download of the audio version of this book. Simply use the code listed below when visiting our website. Once downloaded to your computer, you can listen to the book through your computer's speakers, burn it to an audio CD or save the file to your portable music device (such as Apple's popular iPod) and listen on the go!

How to get your free audio book digital download:

1. Visit www.tatepublishing.com and click on the e|LIVE logo on the home page.
2. Enter the following coupon code:
   7a48-b9b8-403d-5999-3ab2-de2f-c7eb-653d
3. Download the audio book from your e|LIVE digital locker and begin enjoying your new digital entertainment package today!